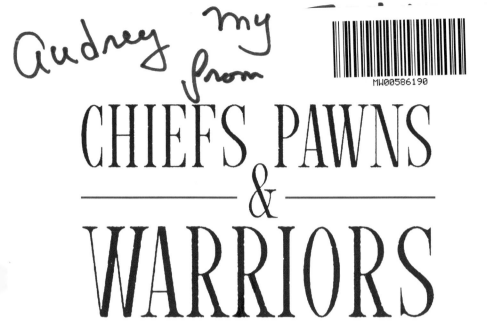

Audrey my from

CHIEFS PAWNS
&
WARRIORS

A MEMOIR OF FIREFIGHTER
Ron Parker's 9/11 Experience

Third Edition

" *NeveR* *FoRgeT* "

RONALD PARKER

9-11-01

Ron Parker

Ron Parker & Associates
BOCA RATON, FLORIDA

Ron Parker & Associates
543 NE 47 Street
Boca Raton, FL 33431
www.AuthorRonParker.com

Ordering Information:
Quantity Sales. Special discounts are available on quantity purchases by corporations, associations, and others. For details, contact the publisher at the address above.

Library of Congress Control Number: 2019900726

ISBN: 978-0-9898055-1-3

1) Personal Memoir
2) American History

Printed in the United States of America

Editing by Danielle Fetherson
Cover image by Karen Spanier
Cover and interior design by www.bookclaw.com

*To my brothers who walked with me
to hell and back, and to those who lost
their way on the return home—
I humbly dedicate this book.*

TABLE OF CONTENTS

ACKNOWLEDGEMENTS

I would first like to thank Megan Basile for assisting me in completing the very difficult task of revising this book. You put up with all of my misgivings and demands for instant perfection with incredible grace without faulting me for my floundered thoughts and words. There aren't enough flowers or thankful gestures that I could lovingly give you to correct my ridiculous meltdowns, rants and raves, and endless wrong doings. Your love for me has never been stronger and I appreciate that agape love.

As for my two sons, Jonathan and Blaze, thank you for allowing me to do my thing and never making me feel bad for dedicating time to write.

Even though you can't speak, thank you Blaze Jr. for helping grandpa.

As for Diesel, my dog and faithful companion, who stayed up late beside me guarding my words and my being, you're the best dog anyone could have.

I also need to thank our cats, Natasha (who passed a few months ago as of the time of this writing) and Dexter (our new addition).

I would also like to thank my very dear friends who also made this book possible, Richard and Ilene Patasnik (especially Ilene who helped me enormously from the very beginning with the help of her daughter Jerri), my number one fan Uncle Buddy Rodney, Edie and Richard Feinstein, Irene and Richard Weinstein, Stan Weisleder.

To all the people who supported me along the way-Mike and Debbie Kevlin, Linda Grillo and her beautiful daughters Jessica and Corinne, Peter and Lori Ferrara, Cousin John, Kevin McFeely, Cousin Ivan, Jim Falcone, Tim Duffy, Mickey Kross, Kimberly Greiger, Beverly and Richard Stapf, Jr., Donna Mcquire, Lillian and Fred Raymond, Palm Beach Captain Matt Willhite, Brett Hill, Robert Calise, Kathy Bien, George Johnson, Danny O'Donavan and my artist friend Chris Pontello—I thank you all so much and I couldn't have done it without you.

I want to thank Karyn Spanier, Kevin's better half, for the amazing photographs.

Thank you to my old friends from Brooklyn, Lenny and Dawn Colletto, Sandy and Mick Goddard and Lance Marz.

And not to be forgotten, two of my oldest friends, Phil "Scoochie" Pascucci and Frank Todisco.

To Steve, Risa, Samantha and Ryan Saffer, my greatest supporters from my new hometown of Boca Raton, Florida.

I would also like to thank the following individuals who also went above and beyond to see this book come to life: Herb and Karen Ellis, Robert Casaburi, John Lapi, Ivan Marcano, Joe McCloskey, Mary E. Thompson, Danielle Fetherson and Briana Ulrich.

To the dozens of others who were part of the process of producing this book and are not named here, thank you, thank you, thank you! Know that your support is not forgoten and your sacrifices have not been in vain.

Never forgetting and always loving my mom, Nancy Parker.

INTRODUCTION

Everyone remembers where they were and what they were doing the moment they heard about September 11, 2001. For those who were in New York at the time, it was the first day back to school for our children. It was a day for us to exercise our democratic right to vote in the primary. It was a bright, sunny, clear and cool fall day that invited you to go outside. But 8:46 a.m. brought a downward spiral into a horrible, terrible, nightmarish day that changed many lives forever. As horrible as it was, my challenge to you is to never forget that day or the lessons that it holds for each of us.

Before I begin talking more about what we can learn from the destruction of the World Trade Center, I want to talk about its history. It was a neighborhood in New York, just like many other city neighborhoods such as Chinatown, Little Italy and Times Square. This sixteen-acre site was known as "Radio Row." It was a small community of a few thousand people who were either ham radio operators or home TV repairmen. People from all over the city would come there to buy parts—such as tubes, diodes, cathodes and even transistors to fix their radios and TVs. Yes, believe it or not, tubes and transistors were used long before microchips or personal computers were even contemplated! The community didn't want their neighborhood as they knew it to be destroyed to make way for the World Trade Center. They eventually lost their case in court. They referred to the towers as "the box the

Empire State Building came in."

The World Trade Center wasn't just the two towers, but a combination of seven buildings. Its foundation was a seventy-five-foot reverse bathtub that dug into the bedrock to keep the Hudson River from seeping into the site—a first-time engineering feat. Japanese architect Minoru Yamasaki, who was deathly afraid of heights, created a design of columns just twenty-two inches wide between the windows, so visitors could lean out while looking out and press against the side of the columns, providing a sense of security.

The towers themselves somehow seemed to be alive. Although the World Trade Center towers contained enough concrete to produce a five-foot wide walkway from New York City to Washington DC, the towers still swayed in the wind, one to three feet in each direction. On the upper floors, such as in the Windows on the World restaurant on the top floor, you could look down at what seemed to be ants. The sun would shine upon you and the ants on the ground would open their umbrellas because it was raining below. If you looked out straight ahead on a clear day, you could see up to fifty miles away with the naked eye. The swaying took a bit of getting used to and it wasn't uncommon to see full glass ripple and spill or to see an aircraft flying well below where you were sitting.

In addition to the 40,000 people who worked in the Trade Center, another 250,000 people would travel there every day, connecting on the PATH trains from New Jersey and the main artery of the New York City transit hub. The U.S. Mall was under the site. With 11.2 million square feet of space, the World Trade Center had its own ZIP Code: 10048. The World Trade Center was *the place to be* in New York City. The right to claim the World Trade Center as a place of employment inspired envy. Most people don't have a workplace that is a city within a city. Live music and entertainment were commonplace in the outdoor mall. Besides its architectural innovations, the towers had other claims to fame. Believe it or not, a French guy named Philippe Petit actually tight-rope walked across the buildings in 1974, and California high-rise rescue firefighter Dan Goodwin successfully scaled the North Tower to demonstrate the possibility of rescue in high-rise buildings.

Now that you know more about what life was like before the World Trade Center was built and what life was like once the towers became part of the New York City experience, you might be wondering what there is left to learn from the towers' destruction on 9/11 and why they should be remembered. Although there were previous attempted bombings on the World Trade Center, an attack of this scale–one that could demolish two 110-story buildings–was considered impossible. The building's freight elevator was the fastest in the world. It could carry passengers and other service items from the ground floor to the top floor in one minute. But once the integrity of the structures was compromised, it took less than ten seconds for each of the 110-story towers to collapse into twenty stories of twisted, mangled steel debris, clouds of smoke, cement ash and papers that spread well beyond the sixteen-acre site. The steel girders that supported the once iconic buildings now looked like a huge pile of twisted Pick-up-sticks.

I remember St. Paul's Church, just across the street from Church and Fulton streets. Its wooden roof and stained-glass-window-accented building was built in 1765. While the New Millennium Hotel—with all its shattered glass windows—was on fire right across the street, and while the trees were burning in the graveyard outside, God protected that church. Not a single pane of stained glass or a single shingle was damaged.

Historically, St. Paul's was one of the first churches in New York City. President George Washington had his own private box and pew there. I remember the church as a place of calm, rest, soulful peace and tranquility for emergency personnel. Cots were placed neatly in rows with homemade quilts and blankets. All had teddy bears on their pillows. I couldn't believe how such a beautiful, quiet oasis was located just a few feet away from the unimaginable hell and destruction surrounding me. While I was in the church, I selected a seat in George Washington's private pew. God had a purpose for that church.

Children from all over the world sent cards and letters by the sacks to the church so that they could be given out to the first responders who sought refuge there. I even received Christmas cards and ornaments. Every Christmas I hang a shell with a pearl on my tree that came from the people of New Orleans' 9th Ward. Each year that I hang the ornament, I think of those people's own suffering during the aftermath of Hurricane Katrina and I pray they're all well.

What do the actions of a New York City Firefighter rushing into the World Trade Center on September 11, 2001 mean to us who responded?

I would say the overriding feeling for those of us who followed the lead firefighters there as our undying respect and the humility for their loyalty, their integrity, their bravery, their professionalism, their unselfishness and willingness to go well beyond what was expected of them.

I am proud to have served with the Bravest of The Brave.

I often think about the Pearl Harbor Memorial where the U.S.S. *Arizona* rests. If you are fortunate enough to visit, you may have the opportunity to meet one of the 2,400 sailors who served on the battleship in Pearl Harbor on December 7, 1941. It was my honor to be part of the December 7, 2013 Pearl Harbor memorial event in Honolulu, Hawaii. I was privileged to meet the eleven remaining sailors who were there that fateful day. The youngest, at the time, was eighty-nine years old. For seventy-eight years, as of the date of this writing, they've told their personal stories of what they witnessed and experienced on that historic day.

They gladly share their personal account of the surprise attack on his ship. If you are a history buff, you may think you know the story. But when he tells you what happened in his own words from his own perspective, the same way he has probably told that story for sixty years, you will have the priceless opportunity to relive it with him before his lips are sealed forever. He didn't ask to be a part of it, but he spoke up nevertheless.

I feel that patriots who have lived through history, like the sailors who lived through Pearl Harbor, have passed the torch to me to continue the legacy of sharing the history of our great land. It is not something I have asked for, but in honor of the 343 firefighters, 37 port authority police officers and 23 New York City police officers who can't tell their stories, I gladly accept the responsibility of sharing how they lived in their final moments. I try to cherish each day that I am alive, and I thank God for everything He has given me.

Just as an attack of the magnitude of what happened at Ground Zero was thought to be impossible, many of us have impossible tragedies that occur in our lives. It can be losing a loved one who kept the family together, a divorce from what you thought was the perfect marriage, a personal attack on your life or a person who robbed you of your confidence or sense of safety. It can be anything.

The stories that unfold in the pages to follow are the stories of a nation that has been knocked down but refuses to stay down. They are the stories of a city that has been physically dismantled while its heart for its people only grows stronger. They are the stories of a man who relied on his training, his brotherhood of firefighters and his faith in God to carry him through the darkest of nights. They are stories recorded in the hope that they inspire you to face the very things that cause you pain and to start living a life that "Never Forgets" the past while still building for the future.

I invite you to connect with me at AuthorRonParker.com to learn more about how I use knowledge of the past to create a better future, and to continue reading to learn more about my past experience with one of America's greatest historical events.

CHAPTER 1

VACATION IS OVER

I waved hello to my favorite bartender, Conner, as I hurriedly entered my favorite watering hole and squeezed past the crowded bar to join my friends. The Jackal was a nondescript little joint nestled between the giant towers that made up the World Trade Center on Hudson Street. As I breezed by, Conner mumbled something about how I owed him because his Red Sox pummeled my beloved Yankees last week. I was already late in catching up with my friends, so I nodded in acknowledgment in the hopes that he wouldn't give me too hard of a time about it.

My dear friends were in the back, gathered around a small round table overloaded with beer and other libations. I could tell that they had started the party without the honored guest—which was me.

It was an unbelievable feeling to know that all of my friends and colleagues, even the ones I hadn't seen in months, had put together this little gala event just for me. It seemed so minuscule compared to the large number of patrons at the bar, but it still meant the world to me. Besides, we were all tech geeks, not party planners and trendsetters. They were sincerely proud of me for being the first to be promoted.

"Cheers! Cheers!" resounded over and over in our small corner.

Collectively, we had worked for years to modify, perfect and incorporate an advanced computerized system that would turn Wall Street on its head by impacting the Forex trading market like never before. Forex was the largest market in the world and traded nearly $2 trillion worth of currency each day. That currency represented all the currency in the world, and my promotion would allow me to change the way it all happened. Cantor Fitzgerald, the investment bank that hired me, didn't quite understand my system or how it would benefit them, but they understood enough to recognize the benefits of hiring me and giving me free rein to use my system to take Cantor Fitzgerald to new heights as an industry innovator. Their new slogan said it all: "The engine of the new market." I was so confident and eager to employ my new trading system.

After a few hours of drinking, my colleagues presented me with a gift that was cleverly wrapped in yellow caution tape, the kind police and firefighters use to cordon off areas of danger. As I struggled to remove the overwrapped package, I realized they had gotten me the greatest gag gift anyone could ever give me. They knew me all too well. My acceptance of Cantor's offer required me to leave my old company on the 5th floor of 77 Water Street and to move to a corner office with floor-to-ceiling glass walls on the 105th floor of the North Tower. I was deathly afraid of heights, so amidst a tumultuous roar from my crowd of friends, I lifted my newly acquired prize—a parachute.

I couldn't believe my eyes. It was a real parachute, not your basic white military one. It was a professional state-of-the-art base-jumping model that deployed a bright red canopy. Embroidered on the strap was my new nickname—"Brave Heart." We all laughed until our sides ached.

I started my job at Cantor on Monday, September 10, 2001. I was treated like royalty. As soon as I stepped off the elevator on the 105th floor, I was greeted by most of the senior partners as well as my new staff and personal secretary. They led me into a beautiful corner office with astounding endless views. The only problem was that I stopped at the threshold of the doorway and had great difficulty proceeding forward into my own office. My abrupt stop caused the entourage that closely followed me to bump into each other. I imagine that the look on my face gave away the cause of my sudden stop as I stared at the two walls of glass facing the City of New York because suddenly everyone remembered they had to attend. Only Gladys, my personal secretary, stayed by my side as I blinked several times and began silently telling myself, "I'm ok. I'm ok."

In an effort to recover from the doorway mishap, I took a deep breath and stared at my feet as I gingerly took one step at a time toward my new chair. After settling in at my desk, I was glad to see that the beautiful leather chair was facing inward toward the rest of the office.

As Gladys offered me soda and juice from the coffee-less coffee room and warned me about the homemade donuts from a co-worker with misguided aspirations of moonlighting as Betty Crocker, I scanned the office, admiring its beautiful and apparently expensive artwork, which tastefully framed the oversized and ornate desk. As my eyes settled on a door to my right, Gladys explained that it was a private executive bathroom complete with shower. I declined her invitation to look at it myself because my heartbeat was just starting to slow down as I recovered from my first glimpse of the two walls of windows that showed just how high 105 stories really is. I didn't want to find out how I would react if I had to look at it again on the walk back to my seat from the executive bathroom. I simply took her word that it existed and suspected that it was just as nice as the office.

I couldn't help but notice the new company mouse pad, designed specifically for my arrival; it read "Cantor Fitzgerald. The engine of the new market." Gladys informed me that my personal belongings would be delivered promptly so I could arrange them in my cavernous office. Shortly thereafter, a box was delivered to my office. It was filled with photographs of my family. Both of my parents and Rex, a French bulldog, were in every photograph. Mom and Dad were especially proud of my accomplishments. I would like to think that Rex was proud too, but as long as he got his treats on time when I returned home in the afternoon, I guessed he didn't really care where I'd been working all day. As I peered down at the bottom of the box, a sense of calm began to overtake me. At the very bottom of the box was the last remaining item—my personalized "Brave Heart" parachute.

A terrible rainy night released an unbelievably beautiful, clear and crisp morning that could only be described as the perfect day. This was the kind of day that I wished I could bottle and spend playing Frisbee with Rex. But, of course, I couldn't skip my second day on the job with, of all companies, Cantor Fitzgerald!

At 7:15 a.m. on September 11, 2001, I paused briefly in front of the gigantic glass structure, looking up to see if I could locate my corner office on the 105th floor. I'm not sure what made me stop; when one got to work this early, why not? Although the building had only four corners, I couldn't be certain which corner surrounded my office because I hadn't looked out at all the previous day, even to see which direction my office faced. I had immersed myself in unlocking and unleashing my new system. The previous day, I hadn't removed my eyes from my computer screen, even to glance outside.

8:46 A.M.

Suddenly, I became a hemorrhage of the glass tower as I clung to the legs of my desk, which hung perilously outside the window of my 105th-story window. I was dazed and confused as my mind instantly replayed how my super-padded high-backed chair had slammed through the impregnable window designed to withstand gale-force hurricane winds as well as the forced strain and twisting that characterized the normal swaying of the superstructure. After shattering the glass, the chair was ejected from the building while I managed to cling to the leg of my oversized desk, which was only inches from falling into the abyss.

I finally convinced myself to loosen my death grip on the leg of the colossal desk long enough to crawl back inside the building before the blunt force trauma to my head caused me to pass out. I awoke coughing and vomiting in total darkness with wet blood covering my head. Due to the heat and deadly smoke that filled everything around me, I was barely cognizant and couldn't understand what had happened or how long I had been lying on the floor of that now completely destroyed office. It felt as if every bone in my body was broken, and the intensity of the pain convinced me that I was still alive. I was scared beyond belief. This was exactly why I was afraid of heights!

Unbeknownst to me, the shattered window that had once threatened my life actually helped spare my life by allowing the fresh air to seep intermittently into my office and keep me alive. Somehow, my right hand remained on the leg of that desk throughout my ordeal. My other arm was lying over my miracle: that gag gift parachute with my name on it: "Brave Heart."

There was nothing to think about. In a matter of seconds, I donned that parachute like a well-seasoned professional skydiver–broken bones and all. But I wasn't quick enough. What I didn't know was that the shattered window admitting fresh air for my survival was also drawing the fiery devil of flames that seemed to start only two to six stories below my office. Craving the oxygen as fuel for consumption and growth, the flames enveloped my office with an unimaginable, rapid and intense heat that seemed to come from Hades itself. It had pushed me outside the 105-story building. Grasping the chute's release handle, I instinctively pulled it and immediately deployed a beautiful, fully enveloped red canopy. At the precise moment when my miracle canopy opened, glass and steel debris from what appeared to be an explosion in the South Tower pierced and slashed through my canopy, accelerating the gravity that pulled on both me and what I had hoped would be my red fabric of hope.

Many weeks had passed at Ground Zero, now referred to as *The Pile*. I was working in recovery mode, painstakingly using a small handheld gardener's rake to search for lost souls. I snagged a small piece of red fabric—a fabric unlike anything I had uncovered previously. As I yanked, pulled and unearthed it, the fabric grew. Most recovered articles were unrecognizable to the naked eye, but the mind sometimes plays tricks. Your concentration is super focused so that you don't miss any small detail that would help you recover someone. Perhaps it was part of a set of fancy drapes or material that adorned one of the many decorated offices, possibly something from one of the shops in the underground mall. The bright red fabric seemed to have nylon cords attached. Further, I discovered a harness with the words "Brave Heart" embroidered on it. Was it possible? Or was my mind playing tricks on me? I was dumbfounded…a parachute? It was a freaking parachute! Although it was torn and burnt, I confirmed that it was a parachute as I gathered it up. When I freed the last bit of the parachute from *The Pile*, I unearthed something: a tattered, mostly destroyed photo of a man playing Frisbee with a dog on a beautiful day. It looked like a French bulldog.

I jumped up and a trail of sweat tickled me as it meandered down the back of my neck. I quickly wiped it away as I blinked three times and tried to take in the different aspects of my surroundings. The red parachute and French bulldog picture had been replaced by a large blue comforter that was draped over me. The longer I sat up, the more I began to register the nightstand with the picture of my two boys, Jonathan and Blaze, on it. My keys and wallet were on the dresser and the light was on in the bathroom. I heard the sound of water running for a shower.

I took a deep breath, exhaled and leaned back on the headboard as I realized that I'd had a nightmare. Everything from running into the bar to getting the parachute gag gift to being thrust out the side of the World Trade Center to finding the picture of the man with the Frisbee and French bulldog…of course, it had to be a dream. *How could I be both the man who plunged to his death and the firefighter who found him?* How could a building that was built to survive hurricane-force winds and designed to sway one to three feet actually snap like a toothpick and crumble to the ground? Crazy things happen in New York, but not things like that. It had to be a dream, right?

As I took another deep breath to calm myself, I noticed the familiar smell that every firefighter knows is the result of a night of tango in the flames. It was then that I realized that I did have a nightmare, but all of it wasn't made-up. The sharp twinge of pain shooting up the back of my legs confirmed that I had been in a terribly serious situation yesterday. As my feet hit the floor, the details of the previous morning came back to me. The previous day had been Tuesday, September 11, 2001.

TUESDAY, SEPTEMBER 11, 2001

My morning routine always varies based on my work schedule. New York firefighters work one of two tours: a 9 a.m. to 6 p.m. tour we call a *9 by* or a 6 p.m. to 9 a.m. tour we call the *6 by*. Everyone knows that regardless of what time your tour is set to start, you are supposed to arrive at least an hour earlier to relieve one of the firefighters who worked the previous shift. So, on the days when I work the *9 by*, I'll make sure to leave home no later than 6 a.m. so I can beat the traffic and arrive at my Ladder 184 Staten Island firehouse by 8 a.m. That's two hours of travel time. If I'm working the *6 by*, I can always leave at 4 p.m. and still make it by 5 p.m. because all the real traffic is coming out instead of going in. But with this being about one week into my three-week vacation, I slept in until around 7:15 that morning.

Jonathan, age twelve, and Blaze, age ten, were having their first day in a new school and I wanted to make sure I got them there on time. I started their morning by making them breakfast. It was nothing fancy, but I did enjoy being able to cook for a normal family of four instead of a firehouse of eleven hungry men. I gave the boys compliments on their new school clothes and walked them to their new school. Then I turned around to come right back to the house.

Seventeen years with the FDNY had trained me well for three weeks as a house-husband. In between runs, down at the firehouse there was always some kind of committee work we had to do. You were either making the beds, doing laundry, scrubbing shower stalls, shining floors, cleaning pots or cooking for the eleven people who were always in the firehouse each shift. Now that I was off, the committee work continued but in a new location.

Around March we had moved into a new home in New Jersey. We must have visited my cousin and my parents in their New Jersey homes too much because my wife, Judy, desperately wanted to move there too. I didn't take her requests all that seriously until one night she mentioned that we had an appointment the next day to look at some homes with a Realtor she had tracked down. Before I knew it, we had spent the morning and afternoon looking at two or three homes. That evening, we were signing paperwork for our new home. Within a few months, we had successfully relocated the other two residents of our triplex Brooklyn home. I told the residents on the top floor not to worry about paying me back for the past year or so when they hadn't paid any rent. They could just leave. As for my mother-in-law, who lived on the middle level, we found her a nice place at the end of the block.

Moving sounds like a simple process. However, once you start cleaning and packing up every single toothpick, old high school yearbook and baby toy from your pre-teen sons room and transport it to a new location, where you discover that fifteen percent of the stuff you thought you had when you packed is now missing and that you now have a desperate need for items you never needed before, it can become a several-months-long process. So now, a full six months after we had moved into the new home, I was still getting things settled. I even turned down a couple of gigs with my moonlighting job as a limo driver to ensure I could make a dent in my list.

As I began tackling the first item, the phone rang. It was my younger brother, Greg. Even with nine years between us, we have always been pretty close. In total, five of us are living at the time of this writing. Our younger sister, Loretta, was born when I was five and died when I was eight, leaving only my brothers Charlie (a year-and-a-half my senior) and Richie (who was born when I was three). Gregory was born later, around the time when I was ten. Finally, Craig arrived around the time I was twelve years old. Gregory lived in Long Island and it wasn't rare to hear from him. What was rare was the flat tone he used with me on the phone. "Put the TV on. Something's going on."

I turned on the TV and saw the line "breaking news" across the bottom of the screen. I looked at what appeared to be smoke coming out of the North Tower of the World Trade Center. In the top left corner of the screen was the word "live." For a moment I wondered if this was a preview for a new movie about something terrible happening in New York. This seemed to be the season for those types of movies. However, as I flipped through a couple more channels and saw the exact same footage, I knew this was no movie preview. As the reality of the image settled in, I watched the second plane hit the other 110-story building. I knew I was no longer on vacation.

I turned to Judy and told her that I had to go. She immediately understood. By now she was a full-time homemaker, but her twenty years with the American Red Cross had made her familiar with the process of how cities deal with disasters.

As I'd done so many times before when I was in the firehouse and we got a call for a *run*, I dropped what I was doing and ran to my vehicle. This time it was my car instead of the *rig*. The difference was that now that I was leaving from home and I'd been on vacation and didn't have my gear, I wasn't sure what I was supposed to do. Should I have race out to the towers and jump in where I could? Should I have gone to my new Ladder 84 in Staten Island to get my gear, report for duty and go from there? Did I really want to delay getting to the World Trade Center where I knew that my old friends from Brooklyn Ladder 148 were already suited up and on their way to what was sure to be one of the greatest disasters any living New York firefighter had ever seen? But even if I did go to Manhattan, what was I going to be able to offer with no gear, no tools, and no orders? Plus, I was pretty sure there would be no place for me to park the car. I knew that I had to go to Staten Island first.

While I was thinking through which direction I would go next, I was already in the car listening for breaking news updates on the radio and driving as fast as I could on the shoulder of the road with no regard whatsoever for speed limits. As long as there was room for my car to safely get down that median and I knew I still had control of the vehicle, I was going to drive. Between my experiences with driving a chase-truck in my pre-firefighter days, racing to the scenes of accidents to get the job for my collision shop and serving as a backup chauffeur with years of experience driving a rig that was about eight feet wide and at least forty-two feet long, I knew I had this four-door sedan under control, even at speeds of eighty to ninety miles per hour. I wasn't alone in that median either. The other vehicles must have contained firefighters, police officers and other emergency personnel because they were flying down the road with me while the other cars were pulling over to the opposite side of the road. This was a total recall of everyone who had anything to do with the safety of our city.

I decided to take the Outerbridge to Staten Island instead of the tunnel. As I approached the bridge, which allows you to look directly over the mouth of the Hudson River at the famous Manhattan skyline, I could see the towers flaming and smoking and resisting the pull of gravity as their supporting girders were pushed and burned to their physical limits. Now I started driving even faster, pushing to 105 miles per hour.

There is always at least one officer in the firehouse. In our house, it was either one of the three lieutenants or the captain. On September 11th, it was the captain. I was so glad it was him. He had to be at least a forty-year veteran. He was a salty, no-nonsense guy. "Sign into the journal. Get your gear ready," he ordered as soon as he saw me.

Now anybody who walks in or out of a firehouse has to sign the journal so there is a written record accounting for all the activity. I signed "R. Parker RFD" (Ready for Duty) in red ink instead of blue. If this were my normal shift, I would have signed in blue. However, when anything out of the ordinary happens, the name is signed in red.

This was definitely a red kind of day. As other firefighters arrived, they did the same.

"You're a chauffeur?" I heard over my right shoulder as I got my gear ready.

"Yeah, I am," I confirmed. "I can drive a rig—Hook and Ladder."

"You can take a spare apparatus to the site, but wait for orders from the battalion, with guys coming in and finding what to do with them."

I got my first set of orders and they put me in the driver's seat, at least until I got my next set of orders. At least my drive to the firehouse had warmed me up for this next drive. I knew I wouldn't be driving a fire truck because our house didn't have one. Spare rigs were located mainly out of the borough. Besides, our house was more accustomed to responding to car accidents, slip-and-fall accidents and medical emergencies other than fires, so we didn't complain about not having the spare fire truck taking up space in our quarters.

From the talk back and forth over the radio, I gathered that all of the Brooklyn and Manhattan firehouses were depleted of their staff, trucks, and equipment. This meant that not only were dozens of firefighters already on the scene, but there were five boroughs with unmanned firehouses in the event of another attack, a house fire or car accident somewhere else in those boroughs. This is not standard FDNY operating procedure. I knew that we could either be ordered to one of those houses to "back fill" and cover those firehouse areas or be called out to the World Trade Center. At this point, no one talked about Al-Qaeda or even about how it had been a terrorist attack, but when two planes decided to crash into the top floors of two of the most distinct parts of the New York skyline, terrorism is the only explanation that came to mind.

Fifteen to twenty minutes after I arrived at the firehouse, I was reunited with my spare gear and traveling in a pick-up truck with four other firefighters to Rescue 5. From there, we were to join the hundreds of other firefighters from around Staten Island, New Jersey and other places to take a series of buses that would lead us to the ferry that, itself, would take us to the island of Manhattan. None of us had any direction on what to do once we reached Manhattan. For the moment we just knew that we needed to get there.

On the series of bus rides, the firefighters were mostly quiet, somber and almost subdued. We quietly filed onto the buses and took off to our final destination, the Staten Island Ferry terminal. I didn't recognize many guys other than the few who had come from the firehouse with me in the pick-up truck. However, I did notice that some were choked up, really choked up, silently praying, hoping that the tension would somehow be cut. Usually, in the moments before arriving on the scene of a big fire, someone would say or do something funny to ease the tension. Guys were usually chomping at the bit, ready to jump into action and take on the fire or whatever was ahead. Well, not this time. We all knew that serious business was ahead of us. I started wondering whether I had kissed my boys and my wife goodbye for the last time. So, before we reached the Staten Island Ferry, I did something I had never done before.

I was sitting toward the front of the bus but was facing the back of the bus. This meant I could see the faces of most of the firefighters who were jammed into the bus with me. I was looking at everyone's individual face. It was quiet. No one was really talking. There was no muttering, nothing. This was definitely an anomaly. That's when I thought that I had to pray and I guess these guys needed a little prayer, too. I figured that the worst thing that could happen was that someone would give me the kind of look that let me know they wanted to call me an altar boy or everything but a child of God, but that they'd still listen.

They must have been relieved when I stood up on the bus and broke the silence. I said, "Listen, guys, bow your heads for a minute. We don't know what we're doing but we need God's help." I started saying the Lord's Prayer right in front of them, as loud as I could. I heard the words resonate throughout the bus as everybody joined in.

I'm not sure what made me get up there and just pray like that. It wasn't something I'd done before. I am a Christian and I go to church on Sundays and try to do the right thing, but I wouldn't say that I'm a holy roller kind of guy. I just knew that we might never be facing a bigger call than this or we'd all be dead already. So, I just prayed. By the time we finished praying, we were already at the Staten Island Ferry terminal.

Just as we reached the ferry, the towers came crashing down within minutes of each other. I never saw the buildings actually come down, but we were close enough that I knew what happened. Nothing else could have created that sound. Even one hundred trains crashing into each other at the same time couldn't have made that sound. When we all looked up, we saw two columns of cement ash, smoke, and papers fluttering in the wind, all outlining the place where the towers had once stood. We couldn't see the towers…we couldn't see anything. None of us had radios on us, so we couldn't communicate with the team on-site to get more details. All we had were our own personal equipment, hand tools and gear.

Shortly thereafter, the ferry took off toward Manhattan. The ferry glided across New York Bay under a clear blue sky that could only be described as perfect. I knew that the closer we got to Manhattan, the more the iconic Statue of Liberty was supposed to come into focus. However, the beautiful clear blue day was marred by the ominous rolling fog of dark ash, dust, and vapors that radiated from the area where the towers had once stood. We couldn't see well. I paused to ponder how strange it was that just a few hours earlier all of us had been in completely different places, doing many different tasks, chores, and jobs. Now we were gathered together in full gear without using or even seeing a fire truck…and all of a sudden…BOOM! Manhattan… the cavalry had arrived as the ferry slammed me from my thoughts and shook me back to reality and the dock at the same instant. The ferry collided with the Manhattan terminal, creating a loud sound that boldly announced it was time for the boat's anxious and eager passengers to disembark.

As I made my way to the front of the ferry, my mind kept trying to process everything that was going on. Not a single car horn was blowing in the city known for being in eternal gridlock. Not a single bird was chirping. Not a single person was shouting at pedestrians in an effort to promote their upcoming event, political cause or knock-off Rolexes (which I affectionately refer to as *Rulex*). In fact, there was no sound at all. The usual smell of greasy foods from the roach coach street vendors was replaced with the thick, choking smell of fire mixed with smoke and ash. All around me, I felt individual particles of soot and grit flying freely through the air. I knew it was best not to open my mouth to speak unless I had to. I'd experienced the unpleasant taste of ash and grime more than a hundred times before and I didn't feel the desire to relive the experience if I didn't have to.

With all the clues I had from the silence that haunted my ears, the singed smell that assaulted my nose and the gritty feeling on my neck, hands and other exposed skin, I still couldn't believe what my eyes were showing me. Depending on the extent of the breeze, I was able to see four feet ahead of me or twenty feet ahead of me at any given moment. Even during those moments of low visibility, I was able to make out the two to three inches of ash that cloaked the dock and streets like well-polluted snow. The road of ash captivated me as I took my first steps off the ferry and onto the docks, leaving well-defined, indelible boot prints behind me.

As I looked up, I noticed the throngs of silent New Yorkers walking solemnly toward the ferry boat to escape the horror I had yet to see with my own eyes. Each person balanced two to three inches of ash on top of their heads.

Manhattan usually draws people with dreams and aspirations for building the next Fortune 500 company, becoming the greatest Rockette in Radio City Music Hall history or taking the fashion industry by storm. Manhattan is usually full of dreamers, optimists and ambitious souls who are the types to never let setbacks dissuade them and who don't believe in defeat. But as I watched them walk toward the ferry that I was leaving, I didn't see the stubborn perseverance and hope to which I was accustomed. Instead, I saw teary eyes that wore blank looks of disbelief or exhibited outright shell shock.

No way was this the city of Manhattan that I had known my entire life. I'm a Brooklyn native, but everyone ends up on the island at some point or another. I had even worked at a couple of firehouses there over the years. This couldn't be real. The city that was usually so vivacious and full of a kaleidoscope of colors was now reduced to three colors: light gray, dark gray and black. I thought I was on the set of a black-and-white movie.

Suddenly, a woman grabbed my arm, looked into my eyes and said, "God be with you!" No amount of training or experience I'd had since joining the FDNY on February 5, 1984 could have prepared me for this. I had no idea what to expect.

As we walked, we could smell the fires. I got to the corner of Liberty and Church and knew exactly where I was. I had been there a hundred times before. I was standing right under the street signs. The towers should have been right in front of me, not even a couple hundred feet to my left. So much smoke was around me that I couldn't really see or breathe. Most of what I could see was on fire. I was standing still and trying to focus my eyes on what was around me as the wind gently blew an opening in the curtain of smoke. I was able to briefly view the space where the World Trade Center towers were supposed to be. I stood there stunned. I didn't understand why I just saw—well, I couldn't believe what I just saw. I looked up again to re-read the street signs; they still bore the same names I had seen before: Liberty and Church streets. I was stunned because when I looked at what should have been two architectural marvels, I saw about twenty stories of piled-up steel. The pieces looked like Pick-up sticks.

I looked down at my steel hand tool, a *halligan* that we use to pry open doors. Then I looked back up at the leveled building, which would soon become known as *The Pile*. I wondered what we were supposed to accomplish with these tools. When I started my quest to become a firefighter in *Probie School,* we learned how to use tools to force doors, create holes or vent the roof to make the fire less likely to create an explosion. We learned to force open doors with steel tools to rescue people trapped in flaming buildings. We learned to safely navigate large, smoky buildings in complete darkness so that we could help anyone trapped inside and find the flames, allowing the Engine Company to come in and put out the fire. In my more recent days with the Staten Island firehouse, I learned more about wrestling mangled cars to free the passengers trapped inside after horrible accidents. I had even learned how to recover people from terrible train accidents. Yet at that moment, I just didn't understand how any of that experience with those tools would help me take on the wreckage of two 110-story buildings. There was nothing we could do with those tools against all that steel. So, what were we supposed to do?

CHAPTER 2

MOONLIGHTING PREMONITION

When my father was a cop with the NYPD, there was no such thing as moonlighting. You couldn't have another job because the assumption was that if you did, you were in the mob. You had to be doing something wrong. It wasn't allowed. You'd get fired from any type of job. I guess if your family had a business, that might have been different, but for the most part, nobody moonlighted. You just worked when you worked. But this wasn't true for firefighters.

I'm not sure if this was because we were in a different type of organization or because we lived in a different time from my father, but nearly every firefighter I'd ever known had a part-time job that they went to when they left the firehouse. This was especially true if they had kids. It wasn't uncommon for firefighters to work construction or go to school. Mike Wernick was a brilliant guy who attended graduate school to become an architect while working in one of the busiest firehouses in the world. He used to stay up all night with pots of coffee in the basement, building little models in preparation for tests. He actually did become a full-fledged architect while he was a firefighter.

One of the best side gigs I ever picked up was with Hollywood. Kurt, the new chief's aide, asked the members of the 9th battalion if they would like to be in a new movie. He was getting ready to retire and follow his new career as a model/actor and he'd found a role that was a great transition between the two careers. He needed about thirty-five off-duty firefighters for a few days. Knowing that I would be off for the next few days, I quickly volunteered.

We would be paid as the lowest-grade non-official stuntmen–basically, glorified extras. I made the cut and was instructed to report downtown at 6 p.m. the following evening, to the front of 2 Broadway with all my personal firefighter gear in tow. It was probably less expensive to pay us to bring the real gear than to hire real actors and supply them with gear (not to mention drive the city's spare fire trucks, which the fire department provided). So, we reported with some spare city rigs and became the official firefighters in the 1989 blockbuster movie *Ghostbusters 2*.

I had never seen the inner workings of a big-budget Hollywood film, much less been part of one. I was getting a paid part! Thirty dollars an hour was much more than the city was paying me. Not a bad gig. In fact, it was the best side job I ever had...and I have had some shitty ones along the way. Who's complaining? You do whatever someone else doesn't want to do. That's why you got the crappy job in the first place.

Ok, now back to being a star actor...I mean, a glorified scrub extra. We were treated very well by all the staff. We were managed by the *wrangler*, or assistant to the assistant producer's assistant, who had the job of *wrangling* or rounding us up so that we were ready to hurry up and wait. A head count for now, then go help yourself to the large assortment of specially prepared food. There was salad, coffee, candy prepared for the A-listers: Bill Murray, Dan Aykroyd, Sigourney Weaver, Ernie Hudson, Harold Ramis, Rick Moranis, and of course...

me.

Still Johnny-on-the-set in the pecking order of firefighters, I was selected by the senior members to make the crucial beer runs to the all-night deli. Between my hurry-up-and-wait cycles, I was fortunate to meet and talk to Sigourney Weaver (who, by the way, is so much more beautiful in person than she appears in the movies). I was even allowed to take photos of her wearing my helmet, as well as photos with Bill Murray and Ernie Hudson. They treated me as if I were one of them and they were especially interested in my career as one of the city's Bravest.

When they finally decided it was time to shoot my role in the movie, they rolled no fewer than ten cameras from all different angles and platforms simultaneously, with accuracy and professionalism. I was sure they would have captured many of us in one particular scene when all the stars were present and acting in their roles. I guess a lot of the great footage that was shot while I was front and center ended up on the cutting room floor because I definitely wasn't in the final film for long. My film debut wasn't as auspicious as I had anticipated. My Hollywood career was brief, although if you happen to view it on DVD or late-night TV, one hour twenty-six minutes and seventeen seconds into the film, you'll find proof that I earned my pay. There's a headshot of two firefighters looking up. I'm the firefighter on the right. Ta-da! I exit stage left.

During my twenty years as a firefighter, I often worked construction on my off-duty days and abandoned any aspirations of becoming a full-time actor. However, I spent many of my later years driving limos.

One of the easiest limo driving nights I've ever had was also one of the scariest. On July 4, 2000, I was hired to drive an older couple out to dinner so they could celebrate their anniversary and the nation's birthday. The part that made the job so easy was that it was only a four-and-a-half-mile drive from their home to their destination. When I picked them up, I met a really nice guy who had just gotten a promotion and was excited about celebrating his career success, his anniversary and the nation's birthday in style with his lady. That was why he chose to take her to dinner at Windows on the World restaurant atop the beautiful World Trade Center. At 9 p.m. multiple barges would take their positions in the Hudson River and unleash an amazing firework display that would be watched on televisions around the country. However, this couple would see it through the large open windows of the iconic World Trade Center.

When I drive, I usually open the door and let the guests into the car, then drive them to their destination and open the door to let them out. I'll wait around somewhere until they are ready to leave and then repeat the process to take them home. But this time the gentleman invited me to have dinner, on him, at the bar in the restaurant. No one had ever offered me such a generous tip. Since it was my nation that was celebrating a birthday too, I thought I should take a minute to celebrate like everyone else. So, I let them go upstairs while I looked for a parking spot.

Finding a parking spot in Manhattan near the World Trade Center on the 4th of July is about as easy as performing heart surgery with only a bottle of rubbing alcohol and a plastic butter knife. I knew it was my lucky night when I found a spot only a block away that could hold the limo. Because locals and tourists were all over the city, looking for a place to camp out before the fireworks started, cops were everywhere. I noticed an officer standing on the corner near the spot I hoped to claim as my own. The space wasn't near a fire hydrant, but I thought it best to ask before I risked having my work vehicle towed before my gig was over. So, I approached the officer.

"Hi. My name is Ron Parker and I'm a firefighter. My dad was a police officer. He told me that if I ever needed a favor to just ask. Will you be here all night?"

"Yes, I'll be here until the fireworks are over."

"Is it alright if I leave my limo here?"

"Sure, you're fine."

"Thanks! I appreciate it!"

I locked up the vehicle and went upstairs to claim a good spot at the bar, where I could enjoy my free meal and watch the fireworks. It would have been nice to have had my wife and my boys with me, but the food and the view were great and served as a decent consolation prize.

Now, I've never been one to believe in visions, premonitions, séances or anything of the sort, but while I was looking out the window, a sense of panic overtook me. My palms and forehead started to sweat, my tuxedo started feeling tight and like it was choking me, and every bit of my senses was screaming at me to get out of the place. The restaurant was filled with the normal chatter and the clanging of silverware on plates that were being relieved of their food; nothing out of place was going on. It didn't matter because everything in me was telling me to get out of there before the building fell. As a firefighter who, at this time, had over fifteen years of experience running into the very situations that everyone else was trying to run out of, I found that panic at this level was foreign to me. So, I did the only thing I could do; I called the server and reminded him which table was covering my bill, then left a tip and ran back to the limo.

I must have startled the officer because he looked surprised to see me when I quickly unlocked the driver's side door.

"We still have time before the fireworks start. You don't have to leave just now. You're fine."

"Thanks, but I gotta go."

I quickly maneuvered the limo out of its spot and drove several blocks north, away from the World Trade Center. I stayed on Chambers and West streets until I got the call from my passengers telling me that they were ready to leave.

I didn't tell the passengers why I left so quickly. I didn't tell my wife about that moment. But as I stood on the corner of Liberty and Church, looking for the building that had housed the restaurant where I had the panic attack, I was in awe.

I didn't stay there long because a chief suddenly appeared. With wide, bloodshot and teary eyes, he welcomed and thanked us for the quick response, then directed us toward Broadway. These orders puzzled us because Broadway wasn't the most direct path to *The Pile*. I guessed that maybe they wanted to break us up into teams and give us specific tasks. This normally wasn't necessary because every firefighter in the firehouse has an assigned role to play. We discover what our roles are when we report for duty. But there was nothing normal about this situation. Instead of having two or three firehouses report to a scene, this was an all-city/all-borough call of every firefighter, on-duty and off-duty. With thousands of first responders anxious to serve, we needed a plan and a strategy quick. All of us were out on Broadway in front of City Hall while the chiefs worked together to build a new command center that would bring order to the situation.

I later learned that my guess was only partially correct. While a couple hundred firefighters were standing with me out on Broadway, a desperate rescue was taking place at the time. We knew only that we had a direct order from a battalion chief whom we needed to listen to. Without question, they didn't want hundreds of firefighters clambering around because they had limited—if not lost—radio communications with trapped and lost firefighters who had been helping rescue survivors in the stairwell of the North Tower.

One of those trapped firefighters was a friend of mine, Lieutenant Mickey Kross. He was there with thirteen other people—eleven firefighters, a Port Authority police officer, and a civilian secretary named Josephine. They were all trapped between the third and fifth floors after the North Tower collapsed. Outside the tower, all efforts were being made to find these trapped and injured survivors with the faint and limited radio communication available. Inside the North tower, the crew didn't know that the entire North Tower had just collapsed.

The History Channel documentary "The Miracle of Stairway B" describes how the trapped firefighter rescue crew would try to direct the firefighters outside to their location.

"Well, yeah. We're in the North Tower."

And the firefighter responds to them: "Where's the North Tower?"

"What do you mean, 'Where's the North Tower?' We're in stairwell B in the North Tower—copy stairwell B."

The building that had been erect just minutes earlier was now gone. It was a cruel magic trick that had produced a daunting task for the exhausted chiefs, many of whom had just miraculously escaped the tower's quick, deadly tumble with their own lives.

Although I'm sure that none of us would blame the chiefs for not taking a moment to sit down with us and talk us through all the horrific details of what our brothers and sisters were experiencing in stairway B of the North Tower. We were quickly becoming bored and anxious. Don't get me wrong; there was activity, but those of us who weren't part of it yet were the anxious ones. Teams were putting out raging fires and pushing hose lines forward to the Trade Center while the lieutenants were trying to work with the firefighters and captains to deploy strategic rescue teams and get them on their way as quickly and efficiently as possible.

The chiefs were holding us back because they didn't want any of their men to get into more trouble than they could handle at the time. The buildings were on fire, the cars were on fire and the streets were on fire, so the chiefs had all the primary streets blocked and were handpicking guys to go down with hose lines and put out the vehicle fires. They were trying to make a path down more selected streets for us to move into the crushed and flaming towers of death and debris. Until they had a way of determining where everyone was going and a strategy for keeping us safe while we rescued the civilians, we were to stay put.

While the chiefs worked diligently to get communications up and running for a command center, there were men like my friend Jimmy Falcone who served as interim messengers. When the chiefs heard someone had a bicycle that could maneuver around the twenty-five acres of ruins, he was quickly recruited as a messenger. However, that wasn't why he was there.

I played many a great hockey game, as well as a good softball game, with Jimmy. He is a brother firefighter with whom I worked on a lot of tours out on Avenue U in Brooklyn. Jimmy worked as hard as a Mason pouring concrete. He always gave one hundred percent for his fellow firefighters, his family and his friends. He also gave his all to a family tradition that had been handed down from his grandfather to his dad and then to him. He had a passion for sports.

I called him the Pied Piper because he had a wonderful way of inventing and creating new and fun ways for kids to perform hockey drills without getting bored. He ran the local recreation center's roller hockey league. He was a certified referee and instructor who was well-schooled in the rules. He always managed to even out the sides or the score by calling the well-placed penalty shot as time withered off the clock while secretly hoping the game would be brought to overtime. It wasn't ever about winning or losing. Jimmy loved teaching the kids regardless of their ability, and they all knew it and loved him for it. In a short time, he could take kids whom no one wanted on the team, evaluate their talents, help them strengthen their skills and coach them, all while having fun transforming them into superstars. Jim did this easily. All the parents loved his dedication to ensuring that the kids had a great time. He even made the rounds to pick up kids from their homes if they didn't have a ride. This was all volunteer work, but that was the kind of Pied Piper guy he was.

Jimmy was working that day as a member of Ladder 153. As the terrible moments unfolded, Jimmy had to get to the Trade Center quickly. His sister was working downtown within earshot of the World Trade Center and he couldn't get in touch with her because all the phone lines were jammed. One of the brothers was working on his vehicle in front of the quarters that morning and Jimmy quickly assigned him his riding position on Ladder 153. Jimmy notified an officer, grabbed his gear and left the quarters of Engine 254 Ladder 153, then proceeded to the car service on the corner of Avenue U and Coney Island Avenue. His demands for a ride to the World Trade Center were initially met with protest, but the driver finally agreed and started the ten-mile drive to the Trade Center.

He should have arrived within minutes, but the NYPD halted all traffic heading in that direction, reserving passage through the Prospect Expressway for emergency vehicles. Grateful for the gear he'd brought with him, Jimmy immediately fled the taxi and hitchhiked a ride into the city in one of the NYPD cruisers. By the time his chauffeured squad car reached the foot of the Brooklyn Bridge, his journey had stopped again. This time the delay was caused by a report that bridges and tunnels into the city were being targeted for bombing by terrorists. With this news, Jimmy quickly suggested that the officer driving the vehicle re-route to the Brooklyn Battery Tunnel, which was only a mile or so away.

When they arrived, they found an engine blocking the entrance. No one was being allowed through the tunnel, either. Jimmy saddled up next to the chauffeur in the engine and learned that the rest of the Engine Company was dispersed throughout the tunnel for radio relay with the towers. After their brief conversation, the chauffeur looked away for a moment; Jimmy seized the opportunity and suddenly started running toward the mouth of the tunnel. Running downhill wasn't so bad as he passed the bewildered relay radio engine men halfway through the tunnel. However, when he started the upward climb on the other side of the tunnel that opened up to Manhattan, he had to remind himself that he was pushing through the pain to rescue his sister.

In no time, he saw a small jeep-like personal vehicle approaching him from the other direction. The driver was Mattie James, the Uniformed Firefighter Association's Brooklyn delegate. The passenger was the captain of the Engine Company. He had just deployed his men throughout the tunnel in the hopes of completing the necessary relay of information from Brooklyn to Manhattan. They instructed Jimmy to get in the jeep so they could take him back to the Brooklyn side of the tunnel, but he took off again in a flash, like a deranged bumblebee on a mission. As he exited the tunnel on the Manhattan side, Jimmy found an abandoned bicycle and a small shovel that he taped under the bike frame. He proceeded to Ground Zero—now fully mobile.

I caught up with Jimmy late that morning before we were deployed on Broadway. He had received word that his sister was safely out of Manhattan. By this time, he was the official communications liaison of Ground Zero. He endlessly peddled the bike around the destruction to relay and dispatch orders among the chiefs. I told Jimmy that he looked like he was in the French Underground. To make his appointed rounds, he was wearing only his firefighter's helmet, shorts, gloves and boots.

Just about that time, I looked up when I heard the familiar roar of an engine. It wasn't just any engine, but the roar of a Harley Davidson motorcycle making its way toward us through the dense smoke and haze. Pulling up before me and Jimmy was Tim Diffy, another member of the "Watchdawgs," the nickname for Brooklyn Ladder 153.

This is not at all what usually happens on a call. It's a well-orchestrated dance and you have to know what you're doing. Each firehouse is typically the home of one Engine Company and one Truck Company—also referred to as a Ladder Company. The Engine Company is the five-person team that operates the hose and puts out the fire while the Truck Company is the six-person team that goes into the building first to perform forcible entry, rescues, locate the flames and vent the building to prevent an explosion or additional damage from superheat and flames that can't escape.

When the Engine arrives on the scene, it has to find the closest hydrant to the building without passing it, then prepare to go in by hooking up to the hydrant and stretching the line.

Once the Truck Company arrives, its members force their way into a building that does not want to help them put that fire out. The chauffeur stays with the truck and operates the ladder if needed. Often, they may position the ladder to help the *roof man* reach the roof so he can tear a hole in it. This hole provides a place for the smoke, flames, and steam to flood through as they try to hide from the Engine Company as they attack it with the water. Otherwise, the steam, smoke and flames may blow back into the faces of the Engine Company. The Truck team also has an *OV*, or *outside vent* person. This person opens or breaks the back windows to provide additional vents for the fire.

Although the *roof man* and *OV* are solo positions usually assigned to the most experienced firefighters in the truck, the officer and the other two men on the truck go in as a team—*the forcible entry team.*

The *forcible entry team* is the *can man*—usually the junior guy because the position allows him to stay with the officer, who has a fire extinguisher and a *hook.* The other person on this team is the *irons man.* This is the guy who has the break-in tools. He has the axe and the *halligan,* which is that pry bar that can break anything. I've never seen one break. I've never seen one bend. I've seen one get run over by a train, but I've never seen one broken. This guy also has the *k-tool* or the *rabbit tool* that can force the doors pneumatically.

The forcible entry team's primary objective is to force entry as quickly, efficiently and safely as possible–even while under duress and in extremely dangerous, deadly conditions because every precious second counts. Often, the team faces an endless array of cleverly placed, unconventional locking systems. In a multi-cultural state like New York, it wasn't uncommon to come across new European or Asian locks, brought in and professionally installed by immigrants, that impeded our necessary entry to the premises. And just when you thought you had it, you discovered another lock backing up the one you just took off.

Military C-4 explosives weren't included in the FDNY's repertoire, though I'm sure some chiefs would have liked to include the explosive material with the rest of the equipment of the rescue and squad companies. However, we came across some doors and locks that would have rendered even the use of explosives unsuccessful. Some drug dealers even devised illegal traps and incendiary deterrents of their own, such as cleverly hidden balloons filled with gasoline that greeted us when we entered their lair. Many of their homemade devices for keeping out the unwanted could probably be adopted for use on 46th

Street's Jewelers Diamond Way—also known as the Diamond District.

In the firehouse, as well as on *The Rock* (the eleven building Bureau of Training site on Randall's Island), we received frequent and lengthy training on the very serious subject of forcible entry. We were trained and retrained as smooth cat burglars who could bypass intricate locking systems without using brute force. We sized up the severity of the situation to determine how to approach our task. Often, very little damage was done to the door because we attacked only the locking system. Urgency and time were important factors to consider. Some of the master tools we used had been invented by career criminals whose specialty was the art of burglary. These devious self-trained thieves were highly skilled and very intelligent. I sometimes wondered what would have happened if these criminals had used their knowledge to serve— instead of steal from—mankind. If they would have legally patented these devices for the fire, police, and military as well as locksmiths, they may have received large financial rewards, possibly deterring them from pursuing lives of crime.

A career thief was caught with burglary tools, including a *k-tool*, and the arresting officers didn't know what it was or how to use it. The arrested tool inventor asked for leniency; in exchange, he would explain what it was and how he had used it to quietly and quickly bypass the safely guarded doors of the city's inhabitants. This tool is now a staple used by every Truck Company in the city of New York.

A whole lot of action goes on really fast. There's a saying: "It's countless hours of mundane placid days, interrupted by seconds of sheer terror." As I stood on Broadway, remembering the glimpse of *The Pile* I had seen only minutes earlier, I knew that more than a few seconds of sheer terror were ahead of me.

I'll admit that I was probably more impatient than most. I was pacing like a caged tiger, although I knew it was a waste of energy. At the time, I didn't know what was going on and I was ready to move. I took it upon myself to cut through adjacent buildings so that I could see what was going on at the World Trade Center. My dad and I used to run a small soda business on Wall Street for brokerage houses. Therefore, I had learned how to cut through buildings and use the back alleys so that I always had a place to park our old, beat-up van, out of sight of the police, when I delivered sodas using the freight elevators at the back of the buildings. Sometimes I would snake in between buildings to get in more deliveries. Now that all of us were in a holding pattern and didn't know what was going on, I decided this was a good time to make use my old skills. Besides, the police were already upset with all the firefighters collecting in one spot and making it impassable, so I gave them a little more room by leaving.

I knew I couldn't take anybody with me because I didn't even know where I was going and I didn't want to create a stir. So, I acted like I had to go to the bathroom, then snaked my way through three or four buildings. I encountered a lot of dead ends. It took a little bit of doing but at the same time, this was good because these guys were putting out fires in the burning vehicles. By the time I got out on the street, many of those vehicle fires had been extinguished and I could make it past without anybody seeing me. I came out near the US Post Office on the northeast corner of the World Trade Center. I was butted up against the building and cautiously sliding across it because glass, metal, and concrete were falling all over the place. I couldn't really see that well, but I could hear stuff falling and see flames reaching out of the building.

I made it to the corner of the postal building. When I turned, I saw an Engine that was hooked up and pumping across from a World Trade Center tower. That's when I saw maybe thirteen, fourteen, or fifteen floors all on fire from almost three or four windows in. Almost the entire side of the building was on fire. I also realized that I wasn't going to make it inside the building to help because flames were literally everywhere. Glass, debris and all kinds of stuff that I couldn't identify were flying in every direction.

In *Probie School*, there was something called a "confidence course" in which we were blindfolded while wearing full gear. Our masks were blacked out and we were told, "Here's the door. Walk through it and get to the other side. We'll be waiting for you." We were mice in a maze that the instructors had created. All kinds of traps awaited us. Some guys put hooks on the backs of the masks like we were caught on something. We didn't know what was hooked onto our gear. We had to stop, figure out which way to roll around and then unhook ourselves from the bicycle or whatever was stopping us. We had to open locked doors. Floors were missing, and we had to know how to walk on a beam to get across. We had to feel which way the beams were going. We had to squeeze through all kinds of stuff and now we were squeezing through a partially collapsed building. They had everything in there, and we had to finish before we ran out of air. Let me tell you, we had to do it correctly the first time. We didn't have time for error because if we took a long time, we were finished.

We had to pace our breathing because we didn't know how much more we had to climb through. Only the instructors had ever seen the entire course from beginning to end with the benefit of full daylight. And it didn't matter if our buddies, those who had been through it before, tried to give us tips because the instructors often moved the doors, walls, windows and everything else in the maze. The instructors were watching us and silently rating every move we made. As ingenious as the invention was when I was in *Probie School*, no simulations could have prepared me for what I saw on my way to the towers. I can't even imagine how they would simulate something like this.

A friend of mine used to own a bar right across the street from the

World Trade Center. At the time he was calling it "New York, New York." I used to go there after work. So did dozens of people who worked in the World Trade Center or other places in the area. That bar was always packed. Every Friday night, crowds would be looking for dinner, drinks and dancing, while the weekends brought high-stakes card games in the basement. It really was a great place. Something was always going on in the city and the bar was one of the places where things usually happened…but not now. The only things happening at this time were fires, flying ash, falling debris and first responders looking for civilians and other first responders who may have been trapped in the collapsed buildings. All the people who made Manhattan come to life were riding out of the city as fast as they could on ferry boats and anything else that would get them out of there.

CHAPTER 3

BOWELS OF HELL

I cut across the street and saw the Engines pumping water. They were hooked up to the hydrants, so I tried to figure out what Engine Company was there. I looked underneath the truck to see if anyone was nearby.

"Anybody? Anybody? Fireman? Fireman!" I yelled. Nobody answered.

Then I ran across the street, making quick and deliberate movements. I dodged falling debris and crawled over unidentifiable, smoldering heaps. I didn't see a single person as I made my way across what was usually one of the busiest streets in the city. There was usually gridlock, but now I couldn't find one person.

Once I made it to the opposite side of the street, I was right next to the North Tower. All the cars on the curb were on fire, so I looked into the car windows to see if somebody had survived.

"Anybody? Anybody? Anybody here? Anybody…"

I just kept hearing myself say that over and over as I made my way down the street toward the North Tower, stopping every five steps to peer into the cars near me. I didn't find a single survivor in any of those vehicles.

I went back to the Engine and saw that the suction hose was connected to the hydrant and was actively pumping water. This told me that I should find firefighters holding the other end of the hose and attacking the flames. All I had to do was follow the hose to find them. But I couldn't make it into the building. I tried many times from different angles, but instead of doorways and hallways, there were seventy-five-foot-deep stories of steel lying on top of each other like pancakes. There was barely enough space to look between the layers of steel, let alone crawl between them to enter the remains of what used to be buildings. It was simply impassible. I couldn't see where the hose line had gone, or the firefighters who had hooked it up.

The building's foundation was seven or eight stories deep and the home of the Port Authority of NY & NJ, or PATH as we called it. It operated a train service beneath the World Trade Center that connected about 250,000 people on its Newark-World Trade Center and Hoboken-World Trade Center routes as well as to the New York City Subway trains that picked up passengers at the station. PATH was connected to the building by a concourse and a shopping center known simply as "The Mall at the World Trade Center." So, at ground level, one could go seven or eight stories under.

I had been a member of Truck Companies for most of my career, so I was in search-and-rescue mode. I set my helmet on the debris and figured that if I got trapped in there, somebody would see the helmet. It would work as a distress signal. If a firefighter throws his or her helmet out the window, other firefighters will know that someone's missing and what company that person is from. I was trying to map out where I was and what I was seeing so that when I went back to the other firefighters, I could tell them whether anyone or anything was in that space. If not, they could better use their time and energy to go to other unexplored areas. They would be welcome to do a secondary search, but at least they would know that the primary had already been complete. At this point, I wasn't even sure if anyone knew I was gone. Besides, the reason why they had us waiting was because at the moment they had too many guys without specific assignments.

I crawled into the underground mall. Once I was inside, I saw that the ceiling actually met the floor. There was no space between them. The opening stopped just one hundred feet in. I couldn't get past anything. I couldn't find anything that was discernible other than the steel beams that were supposed to be holding up the building. After a while, I didn't know where up or down was. I had to crawl over something to go down into something. All I could do was look for voids of space where I could crawl deeper into the maze and look for someone. Someone was going to be behind the beam, or someone was going to be…somewhere waiting for help. That's why I had to get there.

I wasn't worried about getting stuck in a dead end or running into trouble in the buildings. I was on a mission to be there for whoever needed help. If anyone asked what I was doing, I was ready to tell them that I was looking for a restroom, but I knew that waiting around wasn't for me. I had to get there. I had to get the job done.

Everything was on fire. Every time I looked around, I couldn't breathe. I couldn't see. I was crawling on stuff. I tried to crawl in farther, but I reached a dead end. I could hear the military jets high above and I could hear the firefighter P.A.S.S. alarms going off, but I still couldn't go any farther inside. So, I turned around and went back outside. There was nothing there. I hadn't found anyone.

I knew that I had been off on my own for too long; it was time to get back to the muster station and rejoin the firefighters waiting for their orders. As I made my way back to the muster station, I took several pictures with the cheap disposable camera some firefighters (like me) keep with their gear. I knew that no one would believe what I was seeing, so I had to snap pictures. I wasn't concerned about taking pictures on the way in, but I made sure that I took several on the way out.

It's not like I could walk back like one normally walks down a street. I had to stop and duck and look at what was in front of me. I had to create strategies for getting over, under, or around the blazing cars and falling debris. I had to do all this with the snippets of vision I could steal in the midst of all the smoke and ash. The whole time I was out there, I wasn't thinking about being afraid. I was too scared to be afraid because I didn't know what was going to happen. Collapses are similar to earthquakes. When something shifts, who knows what else is going to happen? There's a building next door and it might fall on top of the one you're in. But who knows for sure?

I got past the debris and joined the other firefighters at the muster station on Broadway about thirty minutes after I had left. It looked like the chiefs were making progress in creating teams and sending them out. Finally, we got a group and were assigned to some lieutenant I'd never heard of. Each team had its own space to cover. Ours was down Trinity Place right past the church near the North Tower. I recognized Billy O'Connor, a twenty-year vet from my new firehouse, and we quickly partnered up on the walk down to our group's assigned location. Although I had already been there once on my own, I made sure to take a lot more photos to document everything and study it later. Besides, so much was going on that I was seeing things during this second walk that I had missed the first time around—things like cadaver dogs.

Shortly after the attacks, cadaver dogs were out on *The Pile*. They were so confused because the smell of smoke and death was all around them instead of being in concentrated areas. They walked in circles, trying to pinpoint individual people in distress or people who were already deceased. Their handlers wouldn't release them; they stayed close by with the aid of a leash. I imagined that they were concerned about losing the dogs in one of the many crevices that the canines would squeeze into while following different scents. As they walked around, it wasn't unusual to hear yelps of pain and see the dogs quickly lick their paws after exposed pieces of glass or sharp-edged steel had cut them open. I couldn't watch. It was killing me.

Once we reached our assigned area, we used a rope to tie ourselves together by the waist. This was called a *search line*. It helped us stay together, although we couldn't see each other. If you are on your own, it's easy to get disoriented and not know how to get back out but when you're tied to other firefighters and moving in a line, you can better account for everybody and simply back up to get out. When we went into the buildings, we knew that people were in there because we could hear clambering, but I couldn't see much. Usually, when we went in and out of buildings, we had our own Scott air masks. However, we didn't have any this time, as our supplies were limited. So, we were hoping to take a sip of air here and there, keeping our fingers crossed that things wouldn't go south before we could get out of there.

It was hard to see and hard to breathe inside the buildings. It took twenty minutes to go twenty feet because the wreckage was nearly impassible. We would go up over smoldering office furniture and under fallen beams to make our way through the building. But it seemed like no matter what we did, we eventually got caught in a dead end somewhere. It was a much tighter squeeze than either of us imagined. We're both pretty big boys and in good shape, but everything was very tight.

I heard a rescuer scream that he had found somebody. Somebody was yelling, so we definitely had to go farther down, up, around the debris to follow the voice. We all stopped and listened. Visibility was sometimes limited to your hand in front of your face. Somewhere, a firefighter ahead of us barked for a Stokes basket. The message was telephoned from person to person until one was located and passed from man to man. We pushed, pulled and slithered the Stokes basket over the debris toward the person needing help. The rescuers who were closer to the civilian reached down through the shards of glass, the steel rods and the unyielding concrete to free the prisoner trapped underneath. Finally successful, they lifted the person into the basket and secured them so that the backboard and cervical collar would immobilize them and reduce the risk of further injury before they reached the medical team that was standing by. I don't know who it was, but I know the person was alive. I never saw the person we helped because two or three people were in front of me. I was just grateful that we had been able to get the person out to safety.

Every couple of hours, we were able to go outside and get some oxygen and water. Of course, we didn't have a lot of liquid in there, so when we left to wash our eyes, we got some oxygen and then went back in. We repeated that a couple of times, continuing to go down into the piles of danger and debris.

Manhattan has all of these little bodegas everywhere and that's where we went when we needed some food or water to keep us going. We had to do that to survive and we could get only goods that were sealed. Some guys would take those little power bars but that was about it. It wasn't like we were shopping. We may have grabbed a flashlight or batteries or something else that would help, but it wasn't like we were pillaging. We were procuring anything that might be needed for self-survival, knowing we were there for the long haul. We still didn't know if the attack had subsided or—for that matter—what was going on in the outside world.

I don't remember what time it was, but I do remember a woman sitting on the steps in front of Brooks Brothers, which is a fancy men's clothing store with $5,000 plus suits. The young woman might have been wearing scrubs and she was sitting in a lotus position with her hands out, facing the towers. She didn't say anything as I walked past her; she was as motionless as a mannequin. I didn't know who she was, why she was there or what she was doing. But whatever she was doing had a calming effect on me. She seemed to be the only person there who knew what she was doing.

After I passed her, I went back in and kept hearing military jets flying right over our heads. Like supersonic! Zoom! Zoom! Zoom! Hearing bits and pieces of other attacks…Washington, DC, Pennsylvania…not knowing if the White House was hit. We didn't know if more planes were coming to New York. We were hearing all kinds of stuff, but nobody had any *real* information. We kept getting bits and pieces, but we weren't even thinking about that. Instead, we were thinking about what we had to be doing because everybody else had to be doing what they needed to be doing. The military was doing what they had to do, and we had no idea what was going on outside. I just knew that we had to keep searching for survivors who desperately needed our help. Time was of the essence and it was running out.

We knew…the first one could have been an accident…but the second one wasn't an accident. We didn't know it was Al-Qaeda. We suspected it was, though, because back in February 1993 they had planted a truck bomb in the lower part of the tower. They had parked it next to the support column, hoping that one building would collapse into the other. However, the superior US construction crew had built and fortified the building in such a way that the terrorists' plan was ineffective. So, we knew it was them…who else could it be?

Manhattan is the kind of place where you never go to the same fire twice, not in twenty years. It's not like Brooklyn, where you have row after row of frame houses or single-occupant dwellings or the projects. Everybody in the Brooklyn firehouses knows that there's the A line, the B line, the C line, the D line to all the same apartments. You can get used to that. In those high-rises, you usually spend a lot of time lugging your gear and tools upstairs because the elevator is out. By the time you get there, you start getting to work. You start forcing doors, you have to get in, crawl around, and your Spiderman tingly sense is going off all over the place. You're praying that somebody finds this fire. It's getting hot. It's getting dark and your tank is running low on air. That was what I was used to. And what I was crawling through on September 11, 2001 was absolutely nothing like what I was used to.

Most of us had arrived at *The Pile* between 9:30 and 11 a.m., depending on where we were and whether we were on duty when we heard about the towers. The firefighters who were on duty when the first plane hit the North Tower were the ones who arrived first. For those of us who had more personal things on our list for the day, like pressure washing the house, it took us a bit longer to arrive. Yet all of us were there together, working our way through *The Pile*s of debris, putting all of our senses to work in search of people held prisoner in the concrete.

Even late into the afternoon, the sun still shone from its throne in the sky, piercing the lingering clouds of ash with its rays of light. The warm fall weather that had been so inviting just that morning now stood in stark contrast to the day's events. The peaceful calm and silence that marked the day seemed to mock us as we clambered across the fiery landscape. As dismal as the day was for me, I couldn't imagine what it must have been like for the people who were at work fiddling with their computers or going from one office to another when they were quickly enveloped in a slide of concrete.

Regardless of how my throat burned from the ash and smoke I inhaled or how my hands bled from scraping against the angry, broken glass or how much I was sweating and becoming weary from the constant bending and stooping and crawling and digging, I knew I had to keep going. When I got tired, I remembered the cries I'd heard from the first person I helped free from the concrete prison. I didn't want someone else's concrete prison to become their concrete grave, so I had to keep moving.

There were times when I would stand still and try to steady my breathing as I slowly and methodically scanned my surroundings for any subtle movements. It isn't unusual for someone who is trapped to start wiggling a nearby object in the hopes of catching another person's attention. I was also listening intently for any cries for help. I was listening for the sounds of shifting metal or concrete in an area where no one was walking. Or worse, I was listening for a cry for help underneath the very concrete where I was standing.

It was a constant struggle to balance my determination to hurry up and help people with the knowledge that a hasty movement could cause me to overlook the slightest sign of distress or even cause me to make someone's situation worse by shifting the debris and closing up the pocket of air they were using to sustain themselves. How do you act when you know that both your action and/or your inaction may mean the difference between someone living or dying? This is a question I had always considered early in my career, but it was never so relevant as it was now.

Around 5:30 p.m. all of the rescuers were given the order to stay where we were and not to move. At the time, I was about 300 feet away from 7 World Trade Center in a ring of burning buildings. I had all but blocked the fires out of my focus because I was so honed in on the search and rescue. But moments after I received the order to stop moving, 7 World Trade Center—a fifty-two-plus story flame-assaulted building across the street from the towers that was just beside where I was standing—lost its battle with the wind and gravity and crumbled to the ground, sending a fresh crop of cement, steel, glass, dust and ash (as well as spilling its tons of contents) through the air along with a trail of smoke. As I watched it crumble, I held on to the closest North Tower girder in the hopes that it would support me and help me avoid being sucked under the newly created pile. All the dust that was already on the ground was kicked up all over again. With the imminent threat now over, my brother firemen and I continued combing through the piles in search of our fellow New Yorkers in the few hours of daylight we had left.

Around this time, my heroes arrived: the iron and steel workers. These guys were carrying acetylene torches down the street and trying to make their way with what looked like small cranes. I don't know where they got the equipment, but they just came out of nowhere and stayed with us. A common propane flame burns at 3,630 degrees Fahrenheit, but the acetylene torches they were carrying could burn at about 6,330 degrees Fahrenheit. These torches could slice through many types of metal with ease and could quickly weld pieces together to make any kind of makeshift recovery tool we could imagine. These made-on-the-spot tools were much more effective than any gear that firefighters typically carry.

They'd say, "What do you need? What do you want us to cut?" They didn't give up. They were there. They made the tools that we were missing. They were the ones who made an impact. Their eagerness to jump in there with us gave me an extra boost that helped me get through the night. These rugged, hardcore men saddled up and dug in. They took a terrible feed from the horrible smoke and ash permeating their lungs, but they never complained. They worked steadily while sweating, bleeding, and exerting all the energy that a person could possibly expend. These unsung heroes formed the backbone of laborers who have made America great. I will never look at any of our nation's construction workers the same way after I witnessed their sacrifice in the bowels of hell.

As the evening rolled in, more information was available about which personnel were confirmed to be at work and which were still being reported as missing. Two Port Authority police officers were trapped in the South Tower, across the street from House Engine 10, Ladder 10. For possibly the hundredth time that day, we stood shoulder-to-shoulder to form a human chain that traveled through, up, down and all around the debris. There were actually two chains facing each other so that we could safely and quickly pass the two Stokes baskets carrying the injured officers through our hands to the medics. These were two more people we were able to get out of the wreckage alive. They were the very last living people to escape the grasp of the mangled, fiery tomb.

After the men were moved to safety, Billy, who had been working beside me most of the day, continued climbing through *The Pile* and looking for signs of life. This time we came across a dusty gray hose line. We instinctively followed the line to the nozzle and started aiming at the fire all around us. Within seconds, we shifted from being ladder guys who did search and rescue to Engine guys taking on the flames. Every firefighter is trained to do everything, so it wasn't unusual for us to switch tasks as necessary. At this time of night, it was already hard to see, even with the large work lights from the construction crews. So, we thought that we might as well make use of the hose we'd found to stop the flames from sucking up any oxygen that anyone buried beneath the rubble may have needed to survive until we got to them.

Although switching from Ladder work to Engine work wasn't unusual, it was very unusual to find an unattended hose laying around.

No firefighter ever leaves their tools, equipment, or hose line under any circumstances. If a firefighter was having trouble breathing and could no longer handle the hose line, they would rather die holding the hose line than to pass it to someone in another company. That's just our culture. We do what needs to be done at any and all costs. So, the fact that we found the line lying there meant that the men who pulled it off the truck and hooked it up to the hydrant were most likely buried under the carnage like the hose we had unearthed. We didn't see any signs of life while we were there, so I could only hope that the men who had worked that line were already carried away to a hospital.

It seemed like no matter how much water we forced onto the flames, they wouldn't go out. We pushed on and kept trying, but at around 1:30 a.m. Billy and I agreed that we had done all that our bodies would allow us to do. We had been at *The Pile* for over twelve hours, doing search and rescue and fighting flames. We were shot. We were finished. We could no longer hold the hose. We could no longer force our minds or our bodies to do anything.

We turned to crawl back out through the maze we had entered. It took us about twenty to thirty minutes to maneuver through the dark and to follow the hose line back out to the Engine it was connected to. The hose line snaked up and down and round and round. We knew that we were going the right way because we were following the "bumps to the pumps."

When firefighters are going into a building, they have fifty-foot sections of hose they can connect to each other to adjust the hose line length so that it reaches the flames. At the end of the hoses, where they connect to each other, is a braille-like bump. When the two hoses are put together, one has the bump and one doesn't. The bump to the right, or the bump out, is "bumps to the pumps," and the pump is outside in the Engine. If you follow bumps to the pumps, you're going to get out without going the wrong way. So, we went up, down, all around, following the hose out. It wasn't a direct line, and with us being so mentally and physically drained, it felt like the trip back out was taking forever.

Once we made it back onto the street, Billy and I returned to 110 Liberty Street to the new triage center so we could get more water and oxygen. As soon as we got a doctor's attention so that we could get our oxygen, the doctor made an announcement.

"Ok, three strikes, you're out."

"Wait a minute," I said, puzzled. "What are you talking about?"

"You've been here three times."

We hadn't noticed that each time we came to triage to get water and oxygen, the staff had marked our coats with a grease pencil. Our coats already had two marks on them; now that we were back a third time, they were going to ship us out in an ambulance to a full hospital. It was another policy that came down from the chiefs to make sure we all stayed safe. It made sense, but we still didn't like it. We were tired and just ready to go home; however, we knew there was no use trying to fight the protocol, so we rode off in the ambulance.

What we saw at the hospital was almost as somber as what we had just left at *The Pile*. No fewer than thirty unused, clean and empty gurneys in neat rows greeted us at the entrance to the hospital. No one was lying in them. There were no doctors or nurses. Just empty gurneys waiting to be filled with the same people we had been carrying out of the wreckage in Stokes baskets. It had been disheartening to see so many monumental structures crumble before our eyes back at Ground Zero, but now that we were at the hospital, we were faced with the consequences that those compromised buildings imposed on the people who once occupied them. This was almost too much.

We went inside and the team on duty gave us oxygen. They checked our lungs and everything else on us to make sure we were okay. We were both tired and had a few bruises from crawling around the concrete jungle gym, but we were otherwise okay.

When we saw a chief come in with a heart attack, we exchanged wide-eyed looks that made it clear we were thinking the same thing: We had to get out of there. We knew that everything we had experienced that day was the kind of thing that one couldn't forget. But watching a chief who had been out there with us on *The Pile* struggle for his life was simply too much. Decades on the job had trained us to be tough guys who had the strength to take on the challenges from which most people run. But fourteen hours (and counting) of physical and mental challenges, coupled with the emotional pain of seeing one more member of the brotherhood under an attack that we weren't trained to handle, was simply too much to ask us to take on. So, we dodged the doctors and the paperwork for completing a formal discharge. We simply escaped.

We had already been introduced to our firefighters' help team liaison, who was assigned to escort us home. We found him outside and told him we were ready to go. We quickly left the hospital and headed back to our firehouse on Staten Island, where I hopped into my own car and drove back home. This time, I was obeying the speed limit and playing the radio to help me stay awake. I continued to listen for updates. I heard that everyone got out of the North Tower Stairway B. Some of them died but most of them survived, including my friend Lt. Mikey Kross.

It was between 5 and 6 a.m. when I crawled into bed. I don't remember when I fell asleep or when I woke up, but I do remember the terrible nightmare. When I awoke on Wednesday, September 12th I thought that the events of September 11th had been a nightmare.

But when I smelled the unmistakable odor of smoke on myself after I woke up, I *knew* that crawling through the base of the North Tower and helping carry the people in the Stokes baskets hadn't been a dream. It was only the part about working at Cantor Fitzgerald, the company that had lost the most people in the collapse, that was a dream. The sixteen-acre World Trade Center site really had become twenty-five acres of impassible disaster.

CHAPTER 4

COMPETING REALITIES

Life as a firefighter placed me on the edge of two compelling and sometimes competing realities. In one, I was a first responder who lived to run into scenes where chaos, destruction, and mayhem threatened the lives of others. In the other reality, I was a husband and father who lived to put a smile on his family's faces and to protect and provide for them. In the firehouse, I was part of another family, one of firefighters, a brotherhood who understand that whether we were together in the firehouse or inside a flame-enveloped structure, we had taken a vow to protect the civilians of our great city and to look out for each other so we could all survive to fight another fire on another day.

In the Parker house, I was the primary provider now that my wife had retired after over seventeen years of service with the Red Cross, where I had met her. I was also the activities coordinator, the disciplinarian, the family comedian, the handyman's helper, the part-time backup chef, and, generally, the man who did whatever needed to be done. I never would have become a firefighter if I hadn't had a sense of pride in what I did as well as a deep connection to the men who served with me. But I would never trade the honor of being a husband or a father for anything in the world. So, what happens when the demands of my brotherhood start affecting my family?

I met my wife on the city's Fallen Firefighters Memorial observance day, but I never wanted to think about her having to attend one in my honor. Each October, ceremonies are held around the nation to honor the firefighters who had fallen in the past year since the last memorial. It didn't matter whether the firefighter had died from line-of-duty or non-line-of-duty causes. We would honor any active firefighter for their service. Thousands of firefighters from around the city who were off on the date of the memorial ceremony would assemble on the west side of Manhattan, near the river, in their Class A uniforms to pay their respects.

The ceremony was rarely longer than an hour, but it was understood that everyone who wasn't working would be filling the streets, which were blocked off from traffic, to be part of the ceremony. We would line up and listen in silence as the names of the fallen firefighters were read. There was a bell near the person who was reading the names and the bell would be rung five times for each name mentioned. The reading of the names was followed by remarks from members of leadership. Then we would be dismissed to participate in a union-sponsored luncheon of hot dogs, chips, and beer at an off-site location.

The American Red Cross headquarters was one of the usual places to host our luncheon. The gymnasium in the seven-story building was the perfect size to host thousands of hungry firefighters. And as my wife, Judy, learned while an employee there, it is the perfect place to be hit on when you are a pretty little thing who hangs out on the patio outside the building as thousands of firefighters are passing through.

She was definitely number one on the hit parade for that place, I'll tell you that much. Carefully selecting from among all the men who hit on her, she got lucky and picked me. We started dating and one thing led to another. The next thing we knew, we were walking down the aisle together.

Each day that I go to work, there is always risk involved. Judy and our sons, Jonathan and Blaze, understand what I do for a living and that I can get hurt, or worse, while I'm at work. One time I accidentally rolled up onto a fire with my son Jonathan in the car. He was five or six years old at the time.

I saw plumes of black smoke coming out of the building as I parked in the driveway next to the house that was on fire. I knew that cops and fire trucks would begin arriving soon, so before leaving my car I put Jonathan in the driver's seat and tossed the car keys on the floor beneath him. I told him to blow the car horn when he saw a firefighter and to tell them that his dad was inside the burning building. Jonathan nodded that he understood the instructions. I locked the door and made my way toward the burning building.

I ran up the stoop and into the building through the front door. I heard screams coming from the second floor, so I made my way over the stairs on my left. I crawled up the stairs toward the screaming, but before I reached the top, I noticed flames licking the door of the apartment from which the screams were coming. No way could I get inside to reach anyone. The flames were coming from the open door of the apartment just below them and I knew that the situation would continue to deteriorate quickly. There were also flames all around the stairs. They were burning the hair on my arms and threatening to trap me inside the burning building as well. So, I rolled back down the stairs, ran out the door, and jumped over the railing on the stoop. My goal was to reach the alleyway beside the building closest to the apartment where I had heard the screams.

I ran to a window that I assumed belonged to the same apartment and saw a woman on the second story. She kept yelling for someone to help her children. The lick of flames at the front door let me know that I wouldn't be able to get inside the house to retrieve them. So, I talked the woman into dropping each of her children into my arms. They were small, elementary-school-aged children, so I was able to quickly and effortlessly catch each one.

After I caught the second child and sent them away from the building with a neighbor, I was quickly joined by a sanitation worker who had seen what was going on. It was perfect timing because now the mother had to jump from the window. She wasn't a big woman, but she was bigger than the children. After several minutes of coaxing, she finally swung her legs out of the window and sat on the ledge. With no fire trucks on the scene yet to offer a ladder, and with flames quickly making their way toward the place where she sat, she finally slid off the ledge, letting gravity take her down to where the sanitation worker and I stood.

She fell awkwardly out of the window, so when she landed both she and I fell onto the ground. I think she fractured her ankle, but other than that she and her children were fine. When I made my way back to Jonathan, I found a police officer sitting with him. Jonathan had done exactly what I had asked, and he had seen the entire thing. He had watched his father in action. He was also there with me months later when I was interviewed about the incident on the Les Brown Show. The mother and her two children were there to tell their side of the story and they greeted me with flowers. Not only did Jonathan get a chance to see me work, but he was also able to see an outcome in which the victims survived.

But what was I supposed to say to them when they knew I was leaving home to muddle through the modern hell that was now Manhattan? All of the victims didn't survive this one. By the morning of September 12, 2001, every news network and major talk show on television had replayed the attacks on the towers the Pentagon and the story about the crashed plane in Pennsylvania at least three times an hour. The Internet was full of interviews with teary-eyed witnesses. Blogs speculated about who was behind the attacks and what their motivations were. Every major newspaper around the country had headlines, stories and images that talked about the attacks and the victims. Our president, our mayor and other government leaders had already made public statements requesting support for the victims, providing words of condolence to a grieving nation, and demanding justice from whoever was responsible.

Our entire nation was in mourning. New York's pride was in pieces and my wife and children were looking for family and friends who we knew lived, worked or played in that area. We were all looking for answers that might ease our pain. In the midst of all this, I had to leave my family to rejoin my brothers in search of the men, women and children who we knew were under the rubble. Our search had a great sense of urgency because we knew many would have already died, but we hoped others were still hanging on. At a time when everything you thought you knew about being safe is challenged, there is a natural desire to cling to the ones you feel the most responsible for protecting and to hide them away from anything that might hurt them or even frighten them.

With news of the attacks being the topic of everyone's conversation and in the headlines of every form of media, there was no way that my wife and I could stop our boys from finding out. But after years of convincing them that there were no such things as monsters, what on earth were we supposed to do when they asked what terrorists were? Fortunately, our new hometown in New Jersey didn't have any buildings that were nearly as tall as the World Trade Center, but what could I say to my sons if they ever showed fear of heights or were too afraid to enter skyscrapers? How could I convince them that planes were safe when the most vivid images in all of our minds were of the tail ends of planes protruding from the sides of buildings? And what was I supposed to tell them if the body of someone they knew was pulled from a steel and concrete grave at Ground Zero?

I didn't know how to answer any of these questions. So, when I got up on September 12th and saw my kids, I told them that I was alright and that I was going back into Manhattan with a few friends of mine. I hugged and kissed my family goodbye, then went to my best friend's house to get out of my house before my family had the chance to ask me the questions, I couldn't answer even for myself. Besides, as a firefighter, I'm trained to take action and make unsafe environments safe again, not to sit back and analyze how the environment became unsafe in the first place. The analysis is left for others to do after the main work is done. It was the time for action.

Phil Petti was my best friend and a newly promoted lieutenant who had attended *Probie School* with me. Back in those early days, we were on the same squad. We both got our first assignments in Manhattan. I went to Midtown and he went Downtown. Years later, we both transferred into Brooklyn Ladder 148 and served together for about ten years before Phil was promoted. He was a sharp guy and he definitely deserved the promotion. Yet with the promotion came a transfer to a new firehouse in need of a lieutenant. This meant that we didn't see each other as often as we had when we were in the same firehouse. Still, that didn't stop us from being friends. So, the morning after Dante's Inferno had landed in Manhattan and the FDNY had issued a total recall to every firefighter in the city (and after the nation had been called to be on full alert), I naturally wanted to check on him.

When I got to Phil's house, I found his wife, his brother (who was a Brooklyn firefighter), his mother, and even his father, but no Phil. He hadn't come home the night before and none of them had heard from Phil since the collapse of the towers. He was the covering lieutenant on Ladder 12 on the morning of September 11th. His selfless decisions saved half of his company while they were operating in 3 World Trade Center's Marriott Vista Hotel. Phil's family was anxious for news but was also afraid of what that news might say. The words they spoke were always filled with optimism but the lines on their foreheads, their swollen, crimson eyes and the wastebasket full of tissues told another story.

"Don't worry," I consoled them. "We're going to find Phil. We'll get him. Don't you worry!"

It was already difficult to do search and rescue when you knew that complete strangers needed your help. But now that I knew that my best friend Phil may still have been out there, I had a much more personal reason to get back out to *The Pile* as soon as possible. It was time to go back.

FDNY policy is that once a firefighter has been hospitalized, they are automatically put on medical leave so that they can fully recover before returning to work. Although it makes sense to assume that if a firefighter has been in a situation that was dire enough to land them in the hospital, it would be best for that firefighter to fully heal before returning to work, I had absolutely no intention of sitting around at home hiding behind medical leave while people were still praying to be rescued. So, I called up the medical officer and asked to be taken off medical leave so I could report for duty. The lack of surprise in his voice made me suspect that I wasn't the first person to have called in that day with the same request.

My next phone call was to my firehouse. The day before, I'd had to go to my firehouse before heading to Manhattan because I was on vacation and didn't have my gear with me. This time, I had my gear with me and I wasn't interested in taking the long, scenic route to my Staten Island firehouse before heading to Manhattan. So, I called my firehouse and told them where I was going so that they could make a record of it. Then I drove to Manhattan for the first time since the attacks.

As I approached the area that would soon be known as Ground Zero, I quickly noticed how much more organized everything seemed compared to the day before. The area had been cordoned off blocks away, from Canal Street down (about a quarter of a mile away), and there were now staging areas for security, military and the police. The tunnel and the subway were closed to make sure no one interfered with the search and rescue efforts. None of this surprised me, because the day before I had seen the chiefs of the various first responder agencies working together to put these plans into place. What I didn't expect was to see what the civilians had organized.

After I found a place to park my car, I grabbed my gear and started walking toward the nearest barricade so I could make my way to Ground Zero and report for duty onsite. As I approached the barricade, I saw Asian, Latino, Caribbean, African-American and Caucasian men, women, and children of all ages, standing in a silent crowd and holding signs that featured pictures and names with the words, "Did you see this person? Please call…" underneath. Some of the signs also included the number of the floor on which the person worked and the type of position they worked. Whether they were executives, executive assistants or window cleaners, people were there to represent each one of the World Trade Center's victims. In addition to the signs that people were holding, thousands more signs were posted on ash-covered lamp posts, buildings, and even the physical barricade. Others who weren't holding signs were holding lit candles and photographs of their loved ones. They were holding a vigil. Several were whispering barely audible prayers as I approached.

When I came closer, several people turned to hug me. I noticed that other first responders passing through the barricade, either to leave

Ground Zero or to go out to it, were also being received with hugs, pats on the back, and sometimes solemn rounds of applause expressing appreciation. The crowds were waiting patiently, hoping to receive news about their loved ones. As I walked past them and cleared the barricade, I felt a lump rise in my throat as I realized that while a few of them would receive good tidings, many of them would never see their loved ones alive again. As I pushed this thought out of my mind, a picture of my best friend Phil came to mind. I shook my head and took a deep breath so I could once again focus on the task at hand. This kind of negative thinking wasn't going to make me effective during the search and rescue process, so I had to shake it off quickly.

The path leading up to Ground Zero was much more defined on Wednesday, September 12th than it had been the day before. All of the firefighter rigs, ambulances and civilian vehicles were on the side of the street, positioned into neat piles like junk in a well-maintained junkyard. Although I knew many of the rigs were brand-new, and even the older ones were always meticulously detailed to look like new, they all had the appearance of dirty, discarded rubbish that was crushed, burned, destroyed and now discarded. In one day, the FDNY had lost more than ninety pieces of major equipment, including Hook and Ladder, Engine Company and Rescue Company vehicles. That is more equipment than most major city fire departments have in their entire inventory. Although I had been there the day before, I could hardly believe the amount of destruction I saw before I even reached the buildings that had received the hijacked planes. The damage had crept out blocks away from the location where the planes made impact.

The first things I noticed as I finally approached Ground Zero were the two footpath bridges that had once connected the North and South Towers. One had been completely destroyed by a couple of fires, but the other was still intact. And by "intact," I mean that it was utterly destroyed, but still in one piece. It may have been a random

73

thing to notice under the circumstances, but after walking a few blocks past piles of utterly destroyed vehicles and approaching a site where it looked like a team of wrecking balls had recently had a party, seeing an intact footpath bridge that had barely survived obliteration gave me a glimmer of hope that I would be able to find more survivors—ideally, human survivors.

Everyone's job on Tuesday, September 11th was had been either search and rescue or to put out fires, but with most of the major fires out by Wednesday, September 12th, so we started forming rescue and recovery teams. We couldn't simply leave Ground Zero covered by piles of broken glass, concrete, and steel, so now we were forming bucket brigades to move everything and everyone we found away from the site, piece by piece. To do this, we formed incredibly long human chains by standing shoulder to shoulder and passing buckets of debris from the top of piles out to the perimeter of the site. There, the debris was either hauled off to the nearest dump, kept to for analysis or possibly returned to the company or individual who owned it. Every once in a while, someone would find human remains and direct us to move away from where we were standing so that we wouldn't desecrate the body.

"No, no, no," they would yell. "Don't stand there!"

I think God made me stupid for a reason at that point because most of the time when I heard someone yell at me to step aside and away from a body, I didn't even realize that I was near a body; I didn't know what I was looking at. Everything was covered with gray ash and dust, so there was no blood to be seen anywhere. The smell of burned fabric, rubber, paper and flesh permeated the entire area so it wasn't like a particular smell stood out enough to let me know that I had found someone. I believe that God knew who could handle identifying bodies and who couldn't. I was in the camp that he allowed to be ignorant so that I could keep working. Because I knew that I had problems identifying bodies, I always stepped as gingerly as possible in my sweat-soaked eighty pounds of gear.

We worked silently to find the people who were still alive. We had already found people who had been trapped in crevices when the building fell and we anticipated, or hoped, that we would find more people in similar situations. We also listened for PASS (Personal Alert Safety System) alarms that were going off. The alarms were attached to firefighter air tanks and were designed to go off when the person stopped moving. The ear-piercing sound was heard coming from every direction on the first day. The sheer volume of alarms going off simultaneously made it difficult to focus on one PASS and find the firefighter to whom it was attached. However, as time went on, the shrieking sounds started to fade as the batteries died, the device got wet, or was crushed in the unstable rubble.

If I had still been in my old Manhattan firehouse, the one to which I had been assigned when I first started my career, I would have been one of the first men on the scene and one of the dozens who were crushed when the towers collapsed. It could have been me under thousands of pounds of concrete, praying desperately for a cadaver dog to find me or for a firefighter to wander over to my pile and dig me out. And although it obviously wasn't me who was in that situation, I knew that many of the people who were in that situation were men I had played softball with during the FDNY vs. NYPD competitions, or eaten dinner with in the firehouse, or sat next to in a rig on our way to a call. Some of them were even the same men I'd have words with, going back and forth like big brothers and little brothers who lived to cause each other grief but who would then turn around and give their lives for each other—literally.

The conversation between Engine guys and Truck guys is always about who is better.

"We're the big guys and you're the little guys."

"Cheese eaters!"

"You're the boneheads."

There was always an attitude like one was the older brother and the other was the younger brother. Everything in the firehouse was a competition. There would be an annual softball game or any other kind of sporting event. It didn't matter. There was always a competition. So, once we had enough players, we hosted our first annual roller hockey game with Engine vs. Truck.

We made sure that everyone who wanted to play had a chance to play. If someone didn't have a pair of skates, we got a pair for them. We made sure each team had enough people and we had a lot of fun. Truck won, by the way.

This is Ladder Company 148 and Engine Company 282's first annual roller hockey game in Boro Park, Brooklyn on 53rd Street and Fort Hamilton Parkway. Boro Park has one of the city's few roller hockey rinks and it has been around since the 1940s. This park was actually dedicated for use as a roller hockey park. People used to play on softball fields or any open place with asphalt. I never had hair on my legs because I had slid off the concrete from the time I was eight years old up to the age of eighteen. We didn't play on grass. We played on concrete and asphalt.

The plan was that after we went out to have a lot of fun at the hockey game, we would go to Rocco's Italian Cafeteria and get a few tables set up to feed all twenty of us. Even the guys who came out to watch and who didn't play were going to eat with us. It was only a few blocks away. Anyone who knows anything about Brooklyn knows that Rocco's is *the place to go* for great Italian, and it has been for at least thirty or forty years.

While we were there, we had a few bottles of beer. Some may have had wine or coffee. It was nice. It was in the afternoon, maybe about 3 p.m. At that time, guys started heading out for home. Most of these guys lived in Staten Island, so they wanted to beat the traffic. I didn't rush off. I was actually one of the last guys to leave. Gary was there with me.

While we were there, 85 Truck pulled up with a big-time tower ladder from Staten Island. They had been taken out of service for the day so that they could drive all the way from their Staten Island quarters to *The Rock* between Manhattan and Queens and then go back home. However, they decided to stop at Rocco's. This wasn't a problem because it was on the way. You get off the highway on the Fort Hamilton Parkway exit and Rocco's is right there. They parked the truck across the street from Rocco's, near a bus stop that was maybe a half block away. It wasn't directly in front of the building, but we could see the truck from the front window.

In situations like this, the junior guy is usually assigned to stay inside the rig and safeguard it while the others pick up food to take back to quarters and relieve the company that had been covering the firehouse in their absence. But that isn't what they did. These salty old hairbags decided that every one of them was going to go in there, sit down, and have a lunch break like firefighters *never* do. To make it worse, they were sitting with their backs up against the window, with nobody looking at the rig. All six of them had their backs to the rig. This included the chauffeur, the officer, and the four men. Not one of them cared about their rig.

Gary and I were both chauffeurs, so we knew the drill. We realized that this wasn't supposed to happen. I decided that if none of them went out to the rig by the time I left, I was going to do something. Gary shrugged it off and said that there was nothing we could do, but I was determined that it wouldn't go down like that. So, Gary left and I left, but when I left, I walked toward the rig instead of my car.

Rigs don't have keys. They have a safeguard switch underneath the seat, with buttons and batteries that start it. Only firefighter chauffeurs know where it is—and, of course, I knew exactly where it was. When I looked in the truck, I saw that all the coats, all the helmets, all the masks, and all the tools were in there. I threw on the switch, got in the rig, and left. The firefighters in the restaurant didn't see me leave. I took this truck with a ninety-five-foot tower ladder and they didn't even notice. I drove a few blocks and took a right, then drove a couple more blocks and took a left. I went by a railroad cut and parked the rig under a tree that hid the vehicle well.

I got off the rig and ran because my car was now parked down the block from the restaurant and I had to get back. I ran right past the restaurant. The firefighters were still eating with their backs against the window. They didn't know that their rig was missing. It must have taken me at least eight minutes to run from where I'd left the truck and get back to the restaurant, so that meant it had been over eight minutes since any of the crew of six had turned to check on the rig. I got in my car and drove home, laughing the entire way.

I couldn't wait for each of them to leave that restaurant with their mouths wide open when they realized that their truck was missing. I wasn't there to see it, but I imagine they would have walked around in different directions to look for it, using their radios to talk with each other and relay information. I knew it would take them quite some time to find the fire truck. They didn't want to call the chief because they weren't supposed to be in the restaurant. They didn't want to call the police, but somehow, they waved down a police car and made the officers drive around until they found it. It had to have taken about an hour.

A few hours later, I ended up back in my firehouse. I don't think I was working that night, but for whatever reason, I was back there again. Both the Engine and Truck were out on a call so no one else was in the firehouse except an officer. As soon as I walked in, I heard, "Parker, come up to the office."

"Yeah. What's going on?" I knew that I wasn't working, so I didn't expect much. I just went up to the office.

"You take any fire truck today?" he asked.

I looked right at him. "You know, yup. I sure did."

He thought that I was going to give some excuse or lie. I don't lie. I just told him that I did. I explained that these guys hadn't done what they were supposed to do. I could have denied it because nobody had seen me take it and no one could prove anything, but I didn't see the point in lying.

"You know, I've got chiefs calling. Everybody's calling and it took them forever to find it. Their stuff was missing from the rig…"

I knew right away that he was making up stuff at this point. I knew that no one had taken their masks or any of their gear. But he continued on his rant.

"All of this shit is coming down and I'm the one who has to deal with what you started."

"Look," I said. "I'm not working. So, whatever you want to do." I gave him one of those looks that said I just didn't care. I knew he was lying about the missing equipment to make me feel bad, but I wasn't interested in any of the drama.

"You know something…" I started just as he interrupted me.

"They're going to press charges and you are going to be held responsible for replacing all the stuff that is missing from the truck…" He kept going on and on about all the terrible things that would allegedly happen and cascade down on his head.

I turned around and said, "You know, every firehouse officer's office is filled with volumes and volumes of rules, regulations, charts, codes and all kinds of books that would make you think you're in a law library, but each book is in relation to the fire department. Anything they need to know regarding their job is in one of those books. If they come after me, that's fine. But the shit's going to fall down on them because I'm sure that in one of those books it says that your rig shouldn't be left unattended and not safeguarded by a member at any time. Not to mention that they didn't tell the dispatcher where they were, so they had broken multiple codes before I even showed up. If they want to play the game of pressing charges against me, they are going to have to own up to what they did first. Whatever happens is fine by me because I did take the rig. So, if you want to slap me on the wrist, just do what you need to do."

He turned red like a tomato. He was furious.

"Just get the hell out of here! Get out of here!"

And that was the end of it. Nothing happened and it turned out that nothing was actually stolen from the rig. All the stories about it started to spread and we all knew that they had disrespected their own company by leaving the rig there. After that, there were several times when I took detail assignments at 84 Truck, which was just down the block from 85 Truck. Each time I was in 84 Truck, someone would ask me if I had really taken the truck from 85 Truck. When I was asked, I never denied it. They all thought it was funny. I thought it was hilarious.

"No way! You didn't really do that."

"Yes, I did! What's the big deal? I knew they'd find it…eventually. I just taught them a lesson that they shouldn't leave their rig unguarded. That's all that was."

I would never do anything to put anybody's life in jeopardy. A fire truck in their firehouse was covering the area and they were off the air. It's not like I would have made them late to a call, as someone else was taking their calls. There was no harm and no foul. I just wanted them to give the rig the respect it deserved. It was about honor and living up to the title of being "New York's Bravest." It took years for other salty firefighters and officers to teach me, and I was passing along what I had learned so that they could be even better firefighters than they already were.

CHAPTER 5

THE LIST

Many of those men who trained me and many of those men whom I helped train in my own unique way were the same men I was working tirelessly to find. These weren't just random people whom we were recovering—these were my brothers.

I spent almost the entire day on the bucket brigade, passing five-gallon buckets full of debris. The slow and steady stream of buckets continued twenty-four hours a day and moved through the hands of hundreds of rescue and recovery personnel, including firefighters from all over the country, police officers from hundreds of cities, Port Authority police, New York City sanitation workers, military personnel from all branches of service and even priests, pastors and other clergymen who were ever-present. We were all strangers who, in the face of terrorism that had been designed to steal our hope, banded together to give hope to the mothers, fathers, husbands, wives and children waiting for news about their loved ones.

When we did manage to uncover someone, everyone in the area would stop whatever they were doing. The giant grapplers stopped picking up mounds of debris that were too heavy for humans to pick up. The trucks stopped moving. The generators were turned off.

Everything on that sixteen-acre site stopped. It would be completely silent. I would immediately begin praying for the newly found soul. I would keep praying as I waited for a retrieval basket carrying a body bag and an American flag that I would help pass to the people who were releasing the person's body from the ground.

Some people on the rescue team could precisely identify the exact type of human tissue discovered and could use the angle and position where it was found to help us determine where the rest of the body should be. They would use handheld Global Positioning System devices to mark the area while respectfully protecting its contents. They instructed us to move out of the way so that the experts could carefully and painstakingly dig around the area to fully release the body from the tower's all-encompassing grip. And if the fallen person we discovered was a firefighter, and if we could read the company number on the person's helmet, turnout gear or other items, the chief-in-charge would call the member's company and a detail of men from the fallen firefighter's firehouse would arrive to take out their own in a Stokes basket covered with an American flag. It was always quick. A lot of guys were already there, and they knew the logistics of it. We would wait in a line from deep down inside the debris field all the way out, in any pathway we could. The fallen firefighter would be carried by his firehouse brethren to the top of the hill, where they would wait for an ambulance to give the firefighter his final ride home.

After a while, we all acknowledged that this was no longer a search and rescue. It became a total recovery. The area started to have that unmistakable, rotting stench of decaying flesh and we knew that we probably wouldn't find anyone else alive. Still, we didn't stop hoping that maybe someone had found water, a pocket of air or something in there that had helped them hold on long enough for us to reach them. You always hear about miraculous survival skills that help people beat the odds, but no one ever came out and said, "Hey, we found somebody.

We got somebody over here." As the hours and days dragged on and no new living bodies were found, the reality gradually began to set in. No one else was coming out of Dante's Crushed Inferno alive.

After hours of working on-site at Ground Zero, it wasn't unusual for firefighters to return to their firehouses to get something to eat, get some rest or simply be relieved by someone else reporting for duty on the next tour or work shift. So, when it was my turn to leave Ground Zero and head back to my firehouse in Staten Island, I still had to walk through the same barricades full of people holding vigil that I had passed earlier when I started my tour. Many of the same people I had seen earlier were still sitting there in the dust, hoping to learn that their loved ones' lives had been spared. But from what I had seen over the course of the day, I knew that, at best, they could only hope to receive the bodies of their loved ones if we could positively identify them. As hard as it was for me to watch the bodies of innocent people being recovered from the wreckage, it was even harder for me to look into the eyes of people who reached out to hug me and applaud me for being part of the team that was looking for their loved ones. Not until I was back at the firehouse did I learn that there were even more difficult challenges ahead.

While I was in the firehouse, I learned just how much anxiety a piece of paper could produce. Every so often, each firehouse would post an updated version of something we referred to simply as "the list." It was supposed to be a written record of all the firefighters who had been reported as missing from their firehouses or who were confirmed to be either injured or deceased in the wake of the attack. Although the firehouses were always big on keeping accurate records, it should be remembered that the attacks occurred at the exact time when the evening tour ended and the day tour began. We called it the "change of tours." This meant that it was difficult to know for sure which evening tour guys had already gone home for the day, which had already been relieved by a replacement, and who exactly the replacement was. It was a mess.

During the change of tours, a lot of things can take place. If a firefighter had somewhere he really needed to be around 9 a.m., he might call a fellow firefighter who was scheduled to relieve him and ask that the new guy come in early.

"I have to take my kids to school today and then help my brother fix his car. Can you come in an hour before me?"

So, let's say you were getting out at 9 a.m. and your relief came in at 8 a.m. Sometimes your relief would even come in at 7 a.m. because they wanted to make sure they didn't get caught up in traffic. In fact, it was completely normal for replacements to come in at least an hour before the tour officially changed. Therefore, many of the guys who were scheduled to work from 9 a.m. to 6 p.m. were probably in their firehouses by 8 a.m. and most likely would have been part of the crew to respond to the attacks. However, this is not an exact science. If one of the evening tour guys who was supposed to have gotten off at 9 a.m. was still in the firehouse and heard that a plane had crashed into the World Trade Center, I wouldn't be surprised if he had decided to jump on the rig and go out with the crew because he knew this would be a big one and that more hands would be welcomed. No firefighter ever wants to miss the big one. I'm just certain that none of them knew it would be quite this big or that it might come down on top of them.

To add to the confusion about which firefighters were working, there was something called a "mutual exchange" in which firefighters would trade workdays with someone else. So, let's say Bobby's little girl had a doctor's appointment at 11 a.m. on September 11th and she cried crocodile tears for him to make this one. He might have contacted another firefighter and asked to switch days so that Bobby could make it home in time to hold and comfort his daughter at the doctor's office. Although the official books would say that Bobby was working, there was probably a note in the journal at the housewatch desk of the firehouse, saying that James from the firehouse down the street was filling in for Bobby. It was easy for things like that to get overlooked the first couple of times that the firehouse chiefs were doing roll call and looking for their men. This meant that the chief may have been out there walking past James and looking for Bobby when Bobby didn't even show up that day. But who's to say that when Bobby heard about what was going on downtown, he didn't turn around and run out there as soon as he could, even though he wasn't officially on duty? Firefighters do things like that because we are all just a little off anyway. How else could you explain why we run into burning buildings for a living while everyone else is running out of them?

Here's an example of what I mean by firefighters being a little different, thereby making it difficult to track them. There was an early evening fire on Watts Street in downtown Manhattan, close to the Holland Tunnel entrance. The call came in at the change of tours, when a guy physically relieved another guy by pulling him out of the riding seat with the door open and the truck moving, telling him, "Nah, I'm going. You're out of here." He grabbed him and threw him out. The guy who rode off in the truck was killed along with two other firefighters. A few more firefighters in the rig were injured. In a matter of moments, the guy who had been relieved was saved simply because his replacement physically took his spot at the last minute. It happens.

If someone took a few seconds longer to get into gear than their replacement did, the replacement would relieve the first person and send them on their way. With so many instances like that, it was hard to tell who was missing in the rubble, who had simply passed out on a cot at the nearest firehouse on their way home, who had taken over a shift for someone else or who was already home with their family.

That wasn't the only reason why things were a little confusing. For one of the first times in the history of the FDNY, all of these companies from upstate New York and New Jersey—mostly from New Jersey and Long Island—came in with their rigs and their crews to man the firehouses belonging to all the companies that were at Ground Zero. Although it was great to have someone there to cover the regular gamut of daily calls about fires, car accidents and other emergencies around Manhattan, Brooklyn, Queens and the Bronx, these guys from upstate New York and New Jersey didn't know anything about the protocols for running our firehouses.

They didn't know how to navigate their way around the city like we did, and they didn't know how to deal with the kinds of emergencies that we were used to. If they worked in a city whose tallest building had about eight or ten floors, what were they going to do when they had a report of a fire on the twenty-sixth floor? They weren't conditioned to carry as much as eighty pounds of gear and equipment up that many flights. What did they know about approaching a rear tenement building that required them to go through another building in order to enter? They weren't even used to employing the same type of equipment that we did because this equipment wasn't necessary where they came from.

"These are the tools you'll use. This one you're never going to use, so throw it away. Get back two of these and none of those."

We appreciated them for stepping up and being our new millennium minutemen, but you're only good at what you do and they weren't used to what we did. This was especially true of the firefighters from New Jersey who came from cities that had no high-rises at all. They spent more time responding to car accidents than to fires. They had about five minutes to learn what they needed from the native firefighting companies in between their tours of work at Ground Zero. It was a mess in the firehouses. However, I sincerely thank and commend them for stepping up and putting their lives on the line to fill the giant void at a time when our department most desperately needed help. Again, true American patriotism prevails.

Each time I saw the list, it seemed to bring about more questions than answers. Some lists had 200 names on them. Sometimes the list was 300 or 500 names long. We didn't really pay much attention to the length of the list because we were too busy looking for our friends and family. Many firefighters came from families whose parents, siblings, children, nieces and nephews served in the brotherhood as well. Was this list the "official list"? Had all the facts been collected? Were they sure that this person was dead, or was it possible that the piece of his gear that had been found was something he had dropped as he'd been carried off to the hospital? Maybe he was really in intensive care somewhere and had been overlooked because his name had been written incorrectly on the paperwork.

Things went from bad to worse when I realized I knew forty-five guys on the list. Some of them I knew really well. Some of them I just played softball with or I had shared a tour in their house on a detail with them. "Oh, I didn't know you were a musician. Play that song for me again." But I remembered the guy because I had seen him more than once. The guy said,

"I just got promoted."

"Oh, you got promoted! How did that happen?"

"Yeah, finally hit the books working in the battalion."

You know, I play soccer, I play ice hockey, we set up road trips, baseball games and bus trips…all kinds of stuff. I was always running into guys. Guys I went to *Probie School* with but hadn't seen in a while. It was horrible to see so many of their names on this list. After a while, I didn't want to look at the list because I knew too many guys on it.

And after everything I had seen at Ground Zero, at the barricade vigils on the perimeter of the area, and after skimming through a list of hundreds of people who had lost their lives as I searched for the ones I knew, I still had to go home each day and face my family and friends. What on earth was I supposed to tell them? Was I supposed to tell them the unadulterated truth? Should I tell them that being at Ground Zero was horrific? I truly know now what Dante's Inferno was. I saw it. I walked through it. I breathed it and swallowed it. It's embedded in my DNA, seared into my memory forever. I lived it. Ground Zero looked like a nuclear holocaust. It looked like Hiroshima or Nagasaki in August 1945, when the Allies dropped atomic bombs over the cities to force Japan to surrender and end World War II. I mean, the cars in the streets were all crushed, some reduced to the size of a crushed beer can. We were looking at skeletons of cars and trucks and fire trucks and police cars and buildings. We didn't have access to water on the street because the water mains had collapsed, and the sewer lines were broken. The power lines had been cut. I couldn't even imagine it. We were putting out major building fires as a secondary concern—a much later reaction and response never before given by the city's Bravest.

Should I tell them about the hours I spent going through some of New York's largest hotels, forcing open thousands of doors in search of people who may, or may not, have been in their rooms when a huge chunk of the Big Apple collapsed? Fortunately, in most of the rooms, I found dust-coated, neatly-made beds. Yet even in these rooms, there was more work to be done. In each room, shards of half-inch-wide glass were often precariously attached to the window sill, simply waiting for a tremor or gust of wind to launch them through the air like a dart hurling towards a dart board. My detail partner and I would have to take the delicate and dangerous task of removing each piece from the inside of the room. One slip and you (and the teammate holding you half out the window) would be added to the list. Plus, you could injure or kill someone down below. Scores of fire department teams were precariously scrambling all over the place. Every single door was forced open and broken. I remember thinking, 'Who broke in all these doors?' The rooms were probably empty, but we had to check! Check the closets, check under the bed…we would check everything! God forbid you forgot to check something.

Or maybe I should tell my family and friends how I had received detail assignments that had never before been necessary throughout my seventeen years of service with the FDNY—assignments like installing cameras on what may have been the 30th floor of the Millennium Hotel so that every move on the premises could be recorded? Or how FBI agents and people from various government branches, both military and non-military, were crawling the site alongside me, all conducting their own business of investigation?

I certainly didn't want to tell them about how we had lost the best of the best in that killing field. All the rescue companies, all the squad companies, all the truck companies in Manhattan—these guys were high-rise experts and some of the first men on the scene, the ones who went up into the towers to help people out seconds before the entire building collapsed on top of them and their equipment.

As much as I didn't want to go home and talk about all the lives that were lost, there was one family that I had promised to follow up with. I had already told my best friend Phil Petti's family that I would find him for them. I wasn't the one who found his body. I had simply found Phil's name on the list. I knew that he had served in one of the units that would have been early on the scene, but I had hoped that he had miraculously survived. Because this didn't happen, the only thing left for me to do was to stay by his family's side as they prepared to say their final goodbyes and lay him to rest. We all went to Phil's funeral, but it was a dismal and somber blur—another living nightmare.

CHAPTER 6

HOME TRAINING

September 11th completely changed what I thought I knew about the world, what I thought I knew about being a firefighter and what I thought I knew about myself. I was never under any delusions that there weren't evil forces at work in the world. I had learned that from my father's life as a Merchant Marine and an NYPD police officer.

My father was born Salvador Panasedi on the Lower East Side of Manhattan. The area was known as "Little Italy." Both of his parents (and both of my mom's parents) were Sicilian. My father changed his name in 1947, after World War II, to Charles Parker. My Uncle Raymond also changed his last name to Parker. Dad got the name from his godfather, Charles Gazetta, who worked in a small upholstery shop in Bay Ridge. He did it because of the prejudice against Italians and other minorities. There were also a lot of Jews who changed their names around that time. My father went into the phone book and picked out "Parker," a very generic name, and so went from Salvador Panasedi to Charles Parker.

He was a first-generation Italian-America who had been raised by his mother, Mary, and his mother's parents alongside his brother,

Raymond. My father was an excellent athlete. Although World War II had interrupted his life, he had a great opportunity to play college football as well as baseball and had a promising future in sports.

I guess my dad decided to become a cop sometime after World War II. He was a mariner in the Merchant Marines, transporting oil, ammunition, tanks, soldiers or whatever was necessary to support the invasion of France. He was a crew member aboard Liberty Ship.

He saw a great many of his fellow sailors get killed. During his many crossings of the North Atlantic, he saw several ships get blown up right in front of him. His ship was always at risk of attack from submarines or mines. It also faced aerial attacks and even the natural elements of the high seas. He lived through that. He said to me that when they didn't tell the sailors where they were going, the sailors automatically knew they were going to be part of the invasion. My dad said when he woke up that morning in the sunlight, he saw thousands of ships all in a line—or in columns, as he called them. Whatever they did, he made many trips, but the invasion of France was the big one. He said that he remembered the ship right in front of his exploding from either hitting a mine or being hit by a torpedo. He said, "You could have read the fine print of The New York Times." The death and destruction he saw came at a time when he knew we were at war. My exposure to September 11th came as a total surprise!

When my dad came out of the war, he didn't go to college. He didn't play football or do any of the stuff that he thought he was going to do. He came of age at the tail end of the Great Depression, so after a short career as a mariner who had traveled the world in constant exposure to danger, he decided that a city job would give him a good foundation because it would allow him to stay in the community that he loved. It also offered a moderate amount of protection from the layoffs that were so prevalent at the time. Between the options of becoming a policeman, a firefighter or a sanitation worker, my father found that a career with the police department suited him best. The 64th Precinct in Bay Ridge, Brooklyn was his home for all of his 23 years of service.

Most of the trades at that time were mob-controlled, and those that weren't were run by unions that hired only family members and close friends of people already in the union. My older brother, Charlie, would say, "Look, they're building this new thing in the city. I can get a job. Johnny Wiseguy's brother is going to get me in." Everyone knew that some of the people in those unions didn't really work because the mob-controlled union would cover for them. Thirty people would sign up for work and only twenty-two people would show up. Those who didn't show up probably went to run the numbers, gamble at the racetrack, start drinking and smoking, or do other things that made the mob more money. My father didn't want us to be surrounded by that. He figured that after a while we'd be the ringleaders of that nasty circus. He was smart enough to know the personalities of his children and he kept a watchful eye over us.

"Look, the city job is a great foundation," he often told us. "You can have your house. You'll have your crappy car to go to work. You'll have your house, a couple of kids and your dog and you'll never be more than a month behind on all your bills. How bad is that?"

That was the way he figured it.

He was so excited when he learned that I was going to be a firefighter.

"Wow, that's great!" he had exclaimed.

We didn't know many firefighters because, similar to union positions at that time, it was a nepotism thing. Family and close friends of current firefighters were often introduced to the culture, the tools, the trade secrets and even the chiefs and other leaders who made the key hiring decisions well before they needed the information. So, when it was time to apply for the job, they practically had a guaranteed position. When I officially became a firefighter despite not having a *rabbi* (as the person who helped others get in was often called), my father was exceptionally proud.

I too have always had a sense of pride in having the greatest job on earth and being part of "New York's Bravest." September 11th reminded me that we didn't have that title simply because it sounded good. We earned it. By September 13th, two days after the city as we knew it had collapsed, my new routine of calling into my firehouse and heading into Manhattan was starting to become ingrained into my system. It didn't matter that I was still scheduled to be on vacation. It didn't matter that my muscles ached from lugging my soggy eighty-plus pounds of gear across the twenty-five-acre site for hours at a time. It didn't matter how heavy my heart felt each time we recovered another body, or a new list was released in the firehouse. There was still work to be done, and I wasn't going to let anything keep me from it. There were too many people holding vigil at the barricades and too many more in different parts of the nation—and in some cases, around the world—who were anxious to receive the remains of their loved ones so that they could be placed to rest.

By now, hope of finding anyone alive had been replaced by the hope that we would at least find the remains of everyone who was in or near the building so we could return them to their families. Even this was quite the task. When someone is on the eighty-fifth floor when a glass, steel and concrete avalanche falls to the ground, there is no guarantee that the same person will be a good candidate for an open-casket funeral. Our primary goal was to find them so that they could be positively identified and laid to rest. Our secondary goal was to remove all of the completely destroyed debris so that the men, women and children who lived, worked and played in the area surrounding the twenty-five-acre site could soon return safely. Even the stock market was still closed.

To get the job done, we formed more bucket brigades. There were dozens of bucket brigade lines all around the site, snaking across the heaps of wreckage during our recovery efforts. I wasn't the only person who was getting used to the routine. Everything seemed to flow much more easily. The task ahead of us never became easier, but my confidence in our ability to tackle the task certainly grew. It was obvious that the chiefs knew what they were doing and that they had adapted to this ever-changing and dangerous situation very well.

After my experience with viewing the lists in the firehouses the day before, I decided that I would rather take short breaks near the site than go into another firehouse and face another updated list. I simply couldn't take it anymore. I took a break and lay in the atrium of a big glass building that was part of the American Express headquarters. It resembled a big, broken and inverted fishbowl. The glass was shattered and the palm trees that had once served as accent pieces in the classy main lobby were now wrecked pieces of timber. While I lay on the floor and took a breather, I saw three firefighters walk right into the lobby. They were pristine "GQ" firefighters in brand-new gear, with everything ready to rock and roll. Now that we were three days into our recovery efforts, even the *Probies* just out of school had collected more filth than that on their gear. I looked at them and said, "Boy, where the hell have you guys been?" I've never wanted to take back any words more than those.

The trio had just driven non-stop from Seattle, Washington and was ready to work. They had been driving since Tuesday, September 11th and were just now arriving on Thursday. When they asked me if leaving their car in New Jersey was okay, I told them it was fine and not to worry about it. Then I told them where they could find the chief-in-charge. Meanwhile, I couldn't tell you where their car was, but I could tell you that I felt like a horse's ass for what I had said. These guys were the real deal—real confined-space rescue men who had driven 2,860 miles non-stop in about forty-one hours) from their firehouse on the West Coast to the East Coast just to back us up. If I never learned anything else about them, I learned that they were true warriors.

In the firehouse, the chiefs are always the chiefs. They are the ones who usually have at least twenty years of experience. They are the first ones into the fire and the last ones out. It takes a real leader to convince men to run into a burning building with you and to trust you to make all the calls. The rest of us are pawns. We follow the chain of command and do what the chief says, without questions. We act based on our trust of our chief. Yet at a moment's notice, any of us can become warriors. These two firefighters who had made the decision to jump into their cars and drive almost 3,000 miles immediately after learning about the attacks were the epitome of what it means to be a warrior. They inspired me to go back out on *The Pile* and do more work.

If you would have asked me, a week earlier, what I would have been doing on Thursday, September 13th, I would have told you that I would either be doing work around the house or working my part-time job as a limo driver. As a man who lived in the Depression era, my father appreciated the fact that my job's two-days-on and one-day-off schedule gave me the opportunity to pick up part-time work elsewhere for extra funds. A firefighter could paint houses or drive a cab or do any other side work so long as it didn't compete with the time required to work as a firefighter. When he learned of this, he said, "Boy, if I had that job!" As I mentioned earlier, when my father was a cop, there was no such thing as moonlighting. You couldn't have another job because they figured if you did, you were in the mob. And there was really no such thing as overtime. You just worked when you worked and received your regular pay.

My dad was a really wise person who hadn't received a formal higher education. He was self-educated. He loved to read. He read the newspaper, especially The Times. He never gambled in his life, ever. He would go to Atlantic City with my mother when the casino first came out. She would play the slot machine with the nickels that she had saved while he would walk up and down the boardwalk. My father used to walk the neighborhood with the dog. That was it. He loved to walk. He would talk to people.

My father was very, very, very conservative. You would never have known he was a cop. He didn't look like a cop and didn't act like a cop. I think I'd seen him in uniform twice in my life. When cops retire, they have to turn in their badge, their gun and their black ticket book (or summons book) to their captain. When my father returned his stuff, the captain looked at him and said, "Charlie, this summons book…we haven't used these summonses in ten years."

"I haven't used them since I got them," my dad replied.

My father must have given out three summonses in twenty years. He was the kind of guy who would pull you over and give you one of those twenty-minute sermons about how dangerous it was to drive like that.

"I know you were in a hurry and you have to get home, but now you're going to get a ticket. That could be a whole seven dollars. Oh my God, your husband will kill you."

He was that kind of guy.

"Listen, you got to take care of your family, you got to be careful, be extra, extra careful."

His major values were family and pennies. My father was born October 2, 1921 and those were the messages that stuck with him as he grew up during the Depression.

"Please take care of yourself. I don't want to go to an accident."

This was what he said and that was the kind of cop he was.

He spent most of the later years of his career in the precinct. He wasn't out there fighting crime and chronic traffic violators anymore. When you got twenty years on the force, you were basically an old-timer. They simply gave him one of the calmer details of the 64 Precinct, and while the captain was upstairs in his office reading the Daily News, Dad was down in the basement reading his favorite paper, The New York Times. The station always held at least one desk sergeant, a captain and a cop. My dad was the one cop.

I think my dad retired in 1970. He got out at the wrong time because Mayor Lindsay gave raises to the city workers during each of the two years after my dad retired. He missed it and had never received a good raise in his twenty-three or twenty-four years of service.

With each new detail I took while at Ground Zero, my thoughts kept going back and forth between the task at hand and my family. In particular, when our recovery led me to find part of a mouse pad, a picture frame, keys, or any other personal item, I couldn't help but think about how each person in that building had their own story. For all I knew, my father may have pulled over a relative of whoever used to own the comb I found in the rubble. Or maybe the person who once sat in the chair I was removing was the same person I used to run into when I visited my friend's bar, New York, New York. And when I wasn't imagining the story behind each person who was now in the rubble, I was thinking about my own history and how it had led me to that moment.

I grew up in an Italian neighborhood in Brooklyn. It was called Bensonhurst. I had four brothers. Charles (Charlie) was born in November 1953, I was born about eighteen months later on July 12, 1955. Richie was born June 3, 1958 and my sister, Loretta, was born March 7, 1960. I was eight years old when she died three-and-a-half years later, just months before her fourth birthday. My youngest brother, Greg, was born later.

It goes without saying that my brothers and I took full advantage of the opportunity to skip out on doing homework for a while when Loretta was alive. My sister was hospitalized before the age of one and lived most of her life in the hospital for a grand total of almost three years. Upon finishing her backbreaking work as the neighborhood seamstress, our grandmother watched over us after school. Sometimes friends of the family would step up to care for (and control) the three busy boys, as did aunts, uncles and neighbors.

Dad would pick up Mom every day after his tour at the station house. Mom would stand vigil by the front door, waiting for Dad's arrival. To avoid wasting any time, she would run to the car as it pulled up. Once she took her place in the passenger seat, they would trek to the city to be with the only daughter they would ever have. Mom would have done all the housework beforehand and prepared dinner for all of us ahead of time. She would have dinner with Dad much later in the evening, well after we went to bed and were all asleep.

Every night before they went to bed, they made their rounds to hug and kiss us a good night's sleep. Charlie was always up but pretending to be asleep when they entered the bedroom that we shared. He would be waiting and praying for the encouraging news that my mom would tell him about how much better Loretta was doing in response to a new treatment or medicine. I remained quiet and attentively listened to my mom's sweet, loving and encouraging words. Mom and Dad were always by Loretta's side at the very best and expensive Manhattan hospitals. The world's best doctors were there, sharing all of their knowledge and ready to try an experimental treatment on that deadly blood cancer known as leukemia. When Loretta was well enough, we would all call her on the telephone to tell her how much we missed and loved her. Loretta had but one request. She especially loved it when Charlie whistled the Officer Joe Bolton theme song perfectly, without missing a note. Ironically, Officer Joe Bolton was the cop who hosted the daily afternoon *Three Stooges* TV show. My dad, the cop, lived with the other Three Stooges at home.

At the age of three, Loretta came home only two times during the summer for a few weeks. Mom and Dad said she was tired and needed to go back for a little while to get her strength up. Loretta came home for the last time in the period after Thanksgiving but before Christmas. We all thought this was going to be the very best Christmas we'd ever had. The whole family would be together for the first-time during Christmas. Every inch of the house was decorated inside and out with the greatest of lights and decorations. Christmas at our house was the number-one most fantastic holiday, hands down.

Charlie and I were upstairs washing our large toy trucks in the bathtub carwash, making a watery mess all over the bathroom floor. (I used to wonder why the kitchen ceiling would sometimes leak.) Charlie perked up and heard the very unusual early arrival of Mom and Dad on that cold day of December 19, 1963. We had no time to mop up the mess we'd made in the bathroom. We both slid down the banister in a hurry because we knew they could have arrived home only because they had brought with them our baby sister Loretta, just in time for Christmas. When Dad called for the three of us to sit on the couch after he had switched off all the Christmas lights, our hearts suddenly sank. I felt like I had been punched in the gut so hard I could hardly breathe. Endless shrieks, screams and tears filled the Parker house for the rest of the night.

It was many years later before I learned from my mom why we had never taken a real family vacation after Loretta had left us to be with the Lord. After dodging the question time after time, she revealed that my dad personally went to speak to all of my sister's doctors and asked each of them a simple question.

"If I were a Rockefeller, could you have provided any other

treatment that could have saved my little girl's life?"

They all responded with a resounding "no, no way." Everything medically possible had been done for her. Dad said "fine" and thanked them all for their caring, professional services. Then he asked for the bill. He said it would take some time, but he assured them that the bill would be paid in full, all the way down to the last penny. It took Dad sixteen years after his little angel had gone in the ground to make that promise a reality.

A picture of Loretta hung on the handmade Italian Craftex plaster wall between the living room and the dining room, visible from the front porch. Dad always tipped his hat to her upon entering or exiting our home. Every day, Dad recited his morning prayers in her presence. Every time he passed that wall, he looked up at her, said hello and rubbed the Craftex wall. After many years of repeating the welcome, he unwillingly and completely removed the texture of the wall, rendering it flat and smooth. My darling mother, to the day of this writing in her eighty-seventh year, God Bless her, wears a gold locket with Loretta's photo inside it. She never, ever takes it off. This past year just marked the fifty-year anniversary of Loretta's death.

Parents should never bury their children.

Many years have passed, and my Christmases have never been the same. My children, Jonathan and Blaze always ask me why we don't set up the Christmas tree until it's almost time for Santa. All our friends have had their trees, lights and decorations up since the first break in the weather after the Thanksgiving holiday.

"Santa's going to pass up our house if the Christmas tree isn't up and the outside lights aren't on."

"It's almost Christmas. If you don't set up the tree, we're going to turn Jewish and celebrate Chanukah instead and get eight days of presents instead of one day's worth of gifts."

Jonathan and Dad after the big rescue.

*Brooklyn's L 153 WatchDawgs perilous teamwork
as Richie Barnes holds Billy Stores as he helps
Ron Parker with unconscious victim to safety.*

*The view while we extinguished street fires on our walk
to reach the towers on the morning of 9/11.*

Tim Duffy in action as the WTC 9/11 fire biker.

Ron's helmet identifying where he entered the mall at the WTC.

Mike Wernick's rig.

Ron on the remains of Engine 76 from 100 St. in Harlem.

Inside the bowels of the North Tower.

Three days later on West. St. in Front of American Express Building.

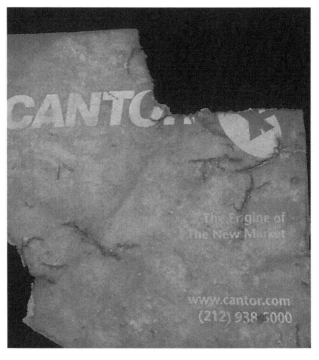

The remains of a Cantor Fitzgerald mousepad.

Part of the plane that hit the Twin Towers.

Parker salutes Lady Liberty aboard Liberty Island Ferry
when statue re-opened.

*Ron and Mickey Kross at the christening
for the U.S.S. New York.*

Ron working at the 9/11 Tribute Museum as a docent.

I explained that we grew up setting up the Christmas tree and lights after December 19th in remembrance of my sister Loretta, who was celebrating in heaven. To this day, that's the way it is in the Parker household and it always will be while I'm alive.

Everybody in our neighborhood worked for a living. I grew up in a Jewish/Italian neighborhood and the Irish were just on the other side in Bay Ridge, the area where my father worked, which was only about four miles away. Our neighborhood had your run-of-the-mill laborers like the seamstresses and those who worked in sweatshops. Then there were the gangsters. Everybody's all mixed up into one space, but we all understand who was who. The gangsters drove the Cadillacs and had the money. They hung out in the 18th Avenue cafés and pool halls that sometimes doubled as bookie joints. The rest of us knew not to go near them. You didn't associate with these people. You didn't walk by the areas where they hung out.

That may have been why my father preferred to work in the Bay Ridge precinct. Bay Ridge was different. It was mostly Irish and the only things that the cops dealt with in Bay Ridge were Friday night drinking and fighting. And although he was a first-generation Italian, my father preferred to not have anything to do with the bad seed Italians in the neighborhood. Back then, the Italian gangsters bothered only themselves and didn't mess with the rest of the people.

My father didn't want us to associate with any of those people or their children. This was easy enough to do because most of them paid to put their kids into private Catholic schools while we went to public schools. I guess they thought they could buy their way into Heaven— the hypocrite personified.

My father did his best to keep us from getting involved with these people. That's why he discouraged us from becoming police officers because he knew that we would end up dealing with them on a regular basis—and maybe even earn their hatred by interfering with their business practices. But with all the energy he put into keeping us away from them, he didn't see it coming when his cousin became deeply involved in their affairs.

Since the 1930s, five Italian American Mafia crime families have been known to orchestrate all of the organized crime in the state and, in some cases, across the nation. The Gambino family is one of them and is credited with everything from construction racketeering to money laundering to prostitution. In 1976, Gambino named his brother-in-law, Paul Castellano, as his successor. My father's cousin Evelyn married Paul Castellano's brother.

My dad had only one brother, so he was very close to his cousins as well—including Evelyn. I saw the pictures and even I could tell that she was a very lovely lady. He had always said that she was a really nice gal. Dad and Mom went to Evelyn's wedding at the Waldorf Astoria but that was the last time my father allowed himself to be in contact with her. He had basically said, "Evelyn, I'll see ya. Have a great life. I'll never know your kids and everybody else." How could he stay in touch with her? He was a police officer and he couldn't risk being around Paul Castellano or anyone associated with him. My dad didn't cross the line. He didn't play both sides of the fence. I don't think I ever met the woman in my life.

No one really held it against her. It was what it was. I learned about her when I saw her in the old black-and-white photo albums that my mom kept. They were the albums with the black backing papers and the little white corners that held the pictures in place. My mother had tons of photos. We'd just go through them and ask questions.

"Who's that?"

"Oh, that's Uncle Al, your father's cousin."

"What cousin? I don't know these cousins."

"Well, that was Castellano."

They told me that my cousin Evelyn lived in a big house somewhere on Ocean Parkway. That's all I knew.

When my mom was a young woman, she collected everybody's photographs. She wasn't around to take them. Grandma had them and she put them in a book for her. Grandma kept them on the dresser or in a drawer.

My mother, Nancy Spitaleri, was also a first-generation Italian-American. She was born in the Bronx on St. Patrick's Day in 1926. I suppose that might be why green is her favorite color. Our whole house was green, or at least accented in green (with the exception of the ceilings). Even the garage was green. If we would have had a dog, he probably would have been green too. That's just how much she liked the color green.

She was raised in Brooklyn and had three sisters, two of whom were twins. There was Anne (my godmother), my mom, Mary, and Jeanie. Her father, my grandfather, was an exceptionally gifted tailor known for his caring nature and generosity. Often, during the Great Depression, he would purchase and deliver food for needy, out-of-work families in the working-class community where he lived. He died of a massive heart attack at age forty-nine. I am convinced that God needed another saint somewhere else.

Nancy was just was like the mother in "Dennis the Menace" or the mom on "Leave it to Beaver," except she was much more beautiful. She also worked ten times harder than they did. She must have done nine loads of laundry a day down in the cellar so that there would be clean clothes for our family of eight: five boys, my mom, my dad and my grandmother, "Nanny," my dad's mother, who lived with us. After doing laundry, Nancy would hang each individual item on the clothesline from the second-floor bathroom window, then iron the clothes once they were dry. Next, she would restock the dresser drawers, make all the beds, sweep, mop and clean the rest of the house.

Our semi-attached brick home had a cellar but not a basement. Nobody had a finished basement. The first floor held a porch, living room, dining room, and kitchen. The second floor held three bedrooms and a bathroom. That was it. Having the eight of us in a three-bedroom, one-bathroom house was definitely interesting on school days. I slept on the porch on the pull-out bed or in the living room on the other pull-out bed. It was tight, that was for sure, but we went to bed so late that it didn't matter. Whenever we were ready for bed, we would pull out the bed and go to sleep. That's how we made do. I like to refer to that experience as being "character-building." It never occurred to us that there could be any other way of life because that was how we grew up.

My mom was great. She would cook and clean and do everything. She would cook the most delicious Italian meals every day, from scratch, on a minuscule budget. Everyone loved to come over and eat anything that she had prepared. Whether it was day or night, guests would come. They especially loved the leftovers. Our refrigerator probably set a world record for the number of times it was opened and closed in a single day. Of all her sisters, aunts, cousins, and even her mother, she was hands down the best cook in the family. Everyone agreed on that.

If you were blessed enough to attend a Nancy Parker Christmas dinner, you would be eating a meal that had taken months to save for and three full days to prepare. You would be surrounded by the complete set of Spode Christmas Collection dinnerware, complete with festive Christmas glasses, candlesticks adorned with red, green and gold candles, exquisite custom tablecloths, and fine cut crystal wine decanters filled to the brim with imported Italian wines.

Our appetizers were fit for a king. They consisted of no fewer than four or five trays of black olives, green olives, Sicilian olives, Greek olives, pimento-stuffed olives, celery, carrots, fresh oven-roasted peppers with roasted garlic, hot and sweet stuffed cherry peppers, pepperoncini, sardines, breadstick rolled Genoa salami, rolled mortadella, rolled baloney for the kids, and rolled ham—all prepared by hand. There would also be fresh prosciutto with melon, fresh mozzarella, tomatoes and basil, fried mozzarella, homemade caponata, eggplant, sliced provolone, gorgonzola, Fontina Val d'Aosta, chunks of Parmigiano-Reggiano, asiago, ricotta salada, pecorino, Romano cheeses, American yellow and white cheese for the lightweights, baked clams, homemade garlic bread with oven-melted mozzarella and famously fresh, crunchy, hot Italian bread from Alba's Bakery on 18th Avenue.

After about an hour and a half of devouring the appetizers, a complete surrender ensued, and guests retreated to the living room or outside to smoke while waiting for round two. This round featured Nancy's famous homemade stuffed manicotti and more wine, but no more bread so that the guests could leave room for dinner. After this round, guests would retreat again to loosen their belts in preparation for round three. This round included oven-baked ham, mouth-watering prime rib, softball-sized rice balls with raisins (for Uncle Ray), or peas that were simply to die for. There would also be fried potato croquettes, stuffed mushrooms, sweet potato mash and a lovely green salad.

Finally, for dessert (for the ones who had left room), after espresso and brown coffee (or at least that's what it was always called), there were honey struffolis with colored sprinkles, walnut tarts, apricot- and strawberry-filled cookies, store-bought cannoli, trays of seven-layer rainbow cookies and every other Italian cookie and pastry known to man. And then there was the fruit. There were so many fruits and nuts that the table looked like a jungle had exploded all over it. It was a truly wonderful dining experience that everyone enjoyed. Nancy worked that kitchen with the precision and speed of an army of chefs, waiters, and busboys. She took pleasure in making sure that everyone from the youngest family member to the oldest was pampered and fully satisfied, and that they left remembering that they were special to her.

CHAPTER 7

THE FDNY JOURNEY

We never went to a baseball game that we had to pay for. We couldn't afford that luxury. Do you want to know how we went to a baseball game? We drank milk by the gallon. If you saved ten milk carton coupons, you received one ticket to some worthless Mets game. We used to drink four or five of them a day to earn those free tickets. Only certain games were available. My father would take us to Mets games because they were free. That was the only way we went.

As children of Depression-era parents, we didn't really know anyone who went on vacation. A couple of kids would go to the Catskills Mountains and have other adventures, but that wasn't our thing. We used to go on day trips to the beach or to Palisades Amusement Park. My uncle had a twenty-eight-foot boat that was like a small cabin cruiser made of wood, but it wasn't the type of thing in which you would take ten people with you. We used it only once. My brother and I would go out on the water with my mother and my father, something like that. My uncle already had a wife and two kids of his own to fit onto the boat, so when we went, our parents took only the two oldest: Charlie and me.

My mother would take us to Bay Ridge to visit the shopping district. I remember that a movie theater called Dyker was right next door to the 64th Precinct, where my father worked. (It's now known as the 68th Precinct.) Mom would take me and my brothers to the movies and Dad would join us later, after he got off of work. Treats like that meant the world to me and my brothers.

One grandmother, my father's mother, spoke fluent Italian and perfect English. She helped my mother look after us. My other grandmother worked in a dress factory. We didn't have any real structure in our lives. When I went to school, I did whatever I wanted to do—and that wasn't always what the teacher was asking us to do. I wasn't a dummy by any means, but if I was taught how to study correctly in a structured setting, I would have done much better in school and probably have achieved greater academic success. I wanted to skate through school and get a seventy—the lowest grade I could get without failing. I just wanted to mind my own business and get by doing the least amount of work possible. I didn't like school very much but I really enjoyed athletics.

My father always had a trunk full of baseballs, bats and footballs and we always played in front of the house. During the summer, we couldn't wait for our father to get off work so we could go down to the beach. He would get off work around 4 p.m. and go in the house to change his clothes. By the time he got back out to the car, we were all waiting on him. About three or four times a week, we would take one of our friends with us on the eighteen- to twenty-minute ride to Manhattan Beach. We would arrive around 4:30 p.m. when everybody was leaving and would stay until 6:30, when we were ready for dinner. Dad tried to take advantage of the opportunity to enlighten and teach us, but we didn't want to listen. We were more interested in crashing against the waves that were always higher late in the day. Sometimes Mom came with us too. It was great!

When we weren't at the beach, we played in our backyard pool. We'd had one of those little metal pools for as long as I can remember. I think our first pool was one of those one-foot canvas pools with the little metal corners. To me, it looked like a recycled army tent that the military had decided to make money off of after the war. Then we got one of those two-foot metal ones. Next, we got a three-foot pool. Finally, we ended up with a four-foot pool that had a filter and all the other gear we didn't need.

Every year, we put it up in time for summer. Then we would take it down. When it was time to put out the pool for the year, we would put all those little bolts down the side, put the things on the top, and fill it with water from our hose (or even borrow a neighbor's hose if necessary). When the summer ended, we cleaned out the liner, undid each of the bolts on each side, rolled it up and put it in the garage.

Many of our neighbors eventually got their own pools, but we were the first. Because all our friends knew that we had a pool, they were always over. Often, we would drag the picnic table and the barbeque out of the garage. I could play ball two blocks away at the schoolyard, come back home, dive in the pool and hang out all day. That part of growing up was really great. But as soon as the barbecue was over, the bench had to go away. And as soon as the summer was over, we quickly put up the pool because we needed the parking space. This gave us more room, making it less likely that we would hit the driveway wall dividing our driveway from the driveway of the home across from ours.

Our semi-attached brick house reached over a driveway to connect with our neighbor's house. The narrow driveway turned my brothers and me into great drivers. Our family had big, powerful station wagons that gave us only an inch-and-a-half clearance on each side before we hit the brick. With a family of eight, it was simply understood that you weren't supposed to break anything because funds were tight and we weren't interested in paying to get something fixed. No one could borrow my father's car, ever. He showed us where everything was located on the car and told us how it worked, but we all knew that if we wanted to drive, we would have to get our own cars or borrow someone else's.

I'm not sure who should get the credit for making my older brother Charlie the best driver I have ever seen. It might have been the tight driveway, my father's training, or a combination of both. My brother could easily have been a winning NASCAR driver. If anybody north of the Mason-Dixon Line ever had a chance, it would have been Charlie. Anybody who has been in a vehicle with him will tell you that. He pulled more than 1,000 automotive stunts that probably should have killed us, but he never had an accident. I have never seen anybody drive like he does. He worked as a delivery boy for a nearby pharmacy and saved for two years to buy his first car at the age of seventeen. He bought a two-door fastback '69 Plymouth Barracuda with a 340 engine. It was a monster car and he used to drive it like a well-skilled maniac.

I will never forget the summer day when he pulled a stunt in the driveway that I never thought would have been possible. Because our house was attached to another house, there were two garages that were side-by-side. Our garage was on the right. To get out, we had to back the car out of the garage and toward the left so that we could straighten the wheel and ride to the bottom of the driveway, up over the little hill where the stoops were located, and then head out onto the street. Near the street entrance were two white columns that we had to avoid. We couldn't make a wide turn there or we would end up hitting the columns. Well, after cleaning his always-immaculate car, my brother lined it up and burned rubber down the driveway, all the way to the street. It was like we were at the race track. That rubber stayed on the concrete for three or four years.

I spent most of my time and all of my summers in the P.S. 205 schoolyard, playing games like *Ringalevio, Johnny on the Pony* and *Spud*, which was also known as *Balls and Guts*. *Balls and Guts* was a game that I made up.

We would start the game by assigning a number to each player. Usually, the largest kid on the court was the person who started the game because no one would challenge him. Next, a small, pink Spalding rubber ball was slammed onto the concrete ground so that it bounced as high as possible. Sometimes the ball would fly two or three stories into the air. While the ball was in the air, all the players ran away to hide while the person who had bounced the ball called out a number. If your number was called, you had to catch the ball before it touched the ground.

If you caught the ball on the fly, it was now your turn to bounce it into the air and call someone else's number. But sometimes kids would run so far away to hide, they wouldn't make it back before the ball returned. If you didn't catch it, you chased it, grabbed it and yelled "freeze." All the players had to immediately stop running and hiding while you picked the closest player to you and launched the rubber ball so that it hit him on the fly. If you missed, you got "asses up." This meant that you stood up against the wall, bent over with your hands on your knees, while every player threw two fastballs each at your butt. With twelve to fifteen players each having two opportunities to hit you, you would often leave the game with welts all over your body. And God forbid you peeked through your legs as you bent over. Unfortunately, many a black eye was rung up by a well-placed eighty-plus-mile-an-hour throw from my neighbors Johnny Corrallo, Joe Palumbo and Tony Puma.

I loved to play roller hockey, but my school didn't have a roller hockey team, so I spent my Saturdays either playing roller hockey in the park or playing stickball, softball or touch football in the schoolyard. But mostly, roller hockey was my thing. Boro Park had a real roller hockey rink that was the most amazing thing in the universe to me. It worked out well that I ended up being a firefighter in that same area for almost ten years!

Of course, I graduated from high school. I just didn't hang out there any longer than I had to. I attended school and, just like I'd done in my early school years, I did whatever I had to do to get by. I didn't like studying. I wasn't really interested in anything. I never really understood how algebra, geometry or other subjects were going to help me, so I put it all out of my mind. Believe it or not, I liked history. I actually went to summer school and got a ninety-nine in history because I was very interested in the subject and I applied myself. The class was taught by a young, creative, caring hip guy who knew how to get my attention. I was satisfied in knowing that I could succeed in school if I was interested in the subject.

As much as I enjoyed that particular class, I was still determined never to go back to summer school again. I had to go, so I went. Most of the teachers gave passing grades to students who showed up. A lot of girls in summer school had PHDs—you know, "phenomenal hair-dos." They could chew gum and twiddle their hair. It was true. Summer school was just a matter of showing up. Even I could do that much! I was relieved when I finally graduated from New Utrecht High School in 1973. This was the school depicted in the opening montage of the TV show "Welcome Back, Kotter."

After high school, I considered joining the Navy, but my dad quickly talked me out of it. The Vietnam War was still going on in 1973 and there was no real indication that it would end any time soon. My dad fought in the war to end all wars and no son of his was going to war—end of discussion. The economy wasn't very good back then and the city was in the process of hiring cops and firefighters, so I didn't look for employment in that direction. I was blessed and got a full-time job elsewhere. My high school job was working for a florist, so once I graduated, I simply took on more hours as they became available. I delivered flowers and learned how to make flower arrangements, but I wasn't very good at it. I was better at preparing the flowers and cutting them. Emeile was a phenomenally gifted florist and was very successful.

I, on the other hand, didn't have the artistic touch. I tried, but God hadn't blessed me with that talent. My claim to fame was borrowing some of the flowers from the over-the-top *avalunedon* floral arrangements meant for dead people and giving them to the most beautiful girls Bensonhurst had to offer, as well as to their grandmothers. Grandmothers always liked me. I remember smoking pot in the van on a far delivery to Long Island, with all these funeral arrangements around me. I stopped to pick up my friends because it was a long trip for a single delivery and I thought some company would be great. Not until later did I learn that driving out to Long Island for a delivery and picking up my friends were two things I shouldn't have done—and two things I would never do again.

We had stopped for burgers and I was driving erratically to make up for lost time. Some of my rowdier friends were horsing around in the back of the van, so the flowers got somewhat mushed and mixed up. When I stood in the parking lot of this funeral home in Long Island and opened the doors, I saw that the arrangements had fallen out of their Styrofoam holders.

Now, these arrangements contained big crosses and hearts with doves in them. Most of them fell out into the parking lot or were mushed. One of my friends asked what I was going to do. I smirked and told him that I was a bona fide professional florist. I started snapping, breaking, and sticking the pieces back into the Styrofoam centerpieces at breakneck speed. I had to get in there quickly before anyone figured out what was going on.

I ran the arrangements into the funeral home and went back to the shop, hoping no one would notice how wrecked the arrangements were or how stoned I was. Emile generally wore a shirt and tie. He reminded me of Floyd, the barber on "The Andy Griffith Show." When I got back to the shop, he waved me in.

"They called," he announced.

As soon as I heard these words, I knew that I was going to be fired. I just didn't know how much drama there would be in the process.

"Yeah, they called and said that they were the most beautiful arrangement they'd ever seen."

I guess the arrangements must have looked pretty good. Or at least they looked good enough for me to keep my job.

Since my days as a faux florist, I went on to have a variety of valuable life experiences. I stumbled through a few odds-and-ends jobs in Brooklyn before hopping on a plane to traverse the country. I became a traveling ad salesman in Los Angeles at around the age of twenty-two. While in the city of Hollywood hopefuls, I jumped head first into the dating game. It wasn't long before I lost miserably and decided to return to Brooklyn, where I could at least enjoy my mom's Italian cooking with no strings attached. By the time I was twenty-six, I was a NYC sanitation engineer. Like my dad, I had become a city worker. Finally, just before my twenty-ninth birthday, which was one year away from the cut-off age, I went to *Probie School* to become a firefighter.

To end up there, I had taken a lot of wrong turns at the right time. I can't say that I was that kid back in school who collected firefighter memorabilia and dreamed about putting out fires. Remember, I was the kid who did just enough to pass, just enough to get by. Not much motivated me back then except sports.

Looking back, I'm still not sure what made me decide to jump through all those hoops to become a firefighter. At that time, firefighters were being hired only once every three or four years, and about 68,000 test takers were competing for one of the 2,500 to 3,000 spots in *Probie School*. At best, this meant that about one out of every twenty-five test takers was going to make it. So, it wasn't about simply "passing" the test, it was about outscoring at least 65,000 other people. Keep in mind that many of these applicants were the sons and grandsons of firefighters, lieutenants, chiefs and captains, so they definitely had a lot more inside information than the rest of us did.

I had to take an eight- to ten-week course taught by firefighters and pass both written and physical tests before I was allowed to attend *Probie School* at *The Rock*. There, I would have the opportunity to learn to be a firefighter. I actually took the test two times. It's not that I didn't plan for it. I had taken the courses and I was good at the physical part. However, it turns out that if someone who was never good at taking tests in school decides to party in bars the night before a test, he doesn't stand a chance. Who knew?

What helped me out was the fact that I had done well on the physical part of the test because of all the walking and heavy lifting in my sanitation job. I purposely ran through my routes to build strength and endurance with no shift relief changes. My daily co-partners loved working with me because all they had to do was drive. I lifted some seven-plus tons of refuse by my lonesome and they were just fine with that. My weekend warrior love of hockey and other sports, which led me to sometimes put in two-a-days at the gym, helped me stay in shape as well. It helped improve my score but not enough to make the cut. I was number 6,108 on the list.

The test was completely revised by the second time I took it. The physical had been modified to give women the chance to join. This time, my combined rating was a near-perfect ninety-nine on the written and over one hundred on the physical. (I completed the course with seventeen seconds to spare and the time was added to my final score in the form of bonus points.) I earned a list number of 305 without the benefit of receiving the five bonus points that were offered to veterans.

The irony, which was the story of my life, was that I was hired off the 6,108 score in the next-to-last class before the city officially killed the list. After twelve additional weeks of fire school at *The Rock*—where I learned tactical firefighting, fire science, engine stretches, hook-ups, hydrants, stand pipes, truck work, ladders, size-ups, forcible entry, roof rope rescues, single slide emergency evacuation, and auto extrications, and where I also received basic EMT training and discovered how to be a loyal pawn who would take orders in a quasi-military organization—I became a full-fledged firefighter in 1984.

The day I became a firefighter, or a *probie* in a firehouse, I knew that I was signing on for a career as someone who would run into the fiery nightmares that everyone else was trying so desperately to escape. I knew that I would be exposed to tragic accidents. I even knew that at times, I wouldn't know what to do right away. But I never knew there would come a day when I would be part of the effort to restore a city that had literally crumbled around us. I never knew that I would lose so many of the firefighters who were my mentors and friends, all at the same time. And I never knew that the events that had tried to destroy the history of my country would also permanently alter my future as a firefighter.

By September 11, 2001, I had seventeen years of service with the FDNY and plans to achieve at least another twenty years. It's not unusual for firefighters to stay on for century-long careers. Most of the chiefs serve for at least twenty years before they even assume that position and then go on to serve for many more years. I was interested in exploring that option until the absurd happened and ushered in one of the most devastating times in my adult life.

9/11 was a disaster for all the brothers of the New York City Fire Department. We all had to deal with it in our own way. The trouble was that no one really knew how to deal with the trauma, grief, loss and never-ending pain. Emotions ran the gamut—some were silent as a mouse in the corner of the church only to become a raging, violent maniac in a moment's notice. The shift between emotions could happen in any place, at any time, and in the company of anyone. The badly beaten remnant of what was known throughout the land as "The Bravest" was a tragic group of lost yet living souls. The entire New York City Fire Department was in a sad state of affairs. It was a miracle that they kept functioning as a cohesive unit, protecting the city they loved.

No division or battalion of therapists and psychiatrists had ever prepared themselves for the most poignant of assignments: working with firefighters and police officers. We are trained to work under a well-defined code of regulations within a defined community. And although we have committed ourselves to serving the public, there is nothing in our culture about being completely open and trusting of someone outside the firefighter brotherhood or our own biological families. Opening up to the people who help you escape from burning buildings or who take care of you when you are sick is one thing Opening up to someone who works in an office that is most often decorated with three or more college degrees is not a normal occurrence for us.

It takes a special person with a lot of patience to earn the trust of salty firefighters, get them to talk about what is tearing them up after having worked at Ground Zero, and then have them implement your ideas for moving forward. Why would someone who has made an entire career out of going into life-threatening disaster areas trust someone who has spent most of their career in air-conditioned offices? That is a tough sell, and not all of the mental health professionals were up to the challenge.

Some of the baptized-by-fire professionals retreated to find other professions. I have personally witnessed this, and I felt so sorry for them that I wished I had never stepped into their office to seek professional help. We were all broken toys. Forget all the professionals who tried to mend us. Despite all the degrees on their office walls, which vaguely described what they were qualified to perform, they could not achieve this task. Although they faithfully and repeatedly tried their best time and again, this was a matter only the Lord Almighty could handle. I now know the meaning of mental paralysis. It is severe depression and loneliness that no one can cure.

September 11, 2001 was only the appetizer. My depression really set in weeks later when the series of funerals started. My very dear friend James "Jimmy" Giberson was forty-three years old and had celebrated twenty years of service to the fire department only six days before his death at the World Trade Center. He was with Ladder 35 and was last seen entering the second tower about ten minutes before it collapsed. Jimmy was the kind of man who lived for his wife and three daughters. He even skipped out on fishing and other events with his friends to spend the day with his daughters. He was the kind of guy you can't help but respect, and I was honored to have had him as my friend.

Jimmy's memorial service was held on Friday, October 5, 2001. By this date, many funerals and memorial services were going on all over the city, especially on Staten Island, which lost the most firefighters on 9/11. I wanted to arrive early enough to enter the church, even if it meant that I had to stand near the back wall. I woke up at 6 a.m. so that I could get out of Manhattan and into Staten Island on time for the 1 p.m. memorial. This wasn't the first service I had attended since September 11th, so I had an idea of what to expect.

All the services and memorials were overcrowded. It seemed as if you were in a subway car during rush hour. The crowds overflowed into the church vestibule and down the steps. Firefighters from all over came to pay their respects, and they lined the walkways and roadways leading to the church. Sometimes the line would stretch a quarter mile in each direction. Each of us wanted to be there to pay tribute to our fallen brother.

The horrific traffic on the way to the funeral gave me plenty of time to admire and duly note the beautiful, clear weather outside. It was almost as clear as it had been on the morning of September 11th. Although I thought my 6 a.m. wake-up time had been early enough for me to secure a spot along the back wall of Christ Lutheran Church so that I could pay my respects to Jimmy and his family, the traffic made it clear that I still hadn't left early enough. I had never attended this particular church, and at the time, it wasn't common to own a GPS that could conveniently re-route your journey when you ran into traffic. The only way I could get there was to follow my handwritten directions, even if they did require me to stay in traffic. I can't even describe the relief I felt when I saw the church steeple ahead.

As soon as I saw that steeple, I stopped looking down at my written directions and simply started following the traffic that seemed to be heading in that direction. Soon I approached the New York Police Department's traffic detail assigned to the funeral. They did a great job of leading us to parking lots and spots near the church. The church's parking lot was filled to capacity. Cars parked on the grass and in other makeshift parking spaces that were usually illegal. The lots were typically reserved for family and friends, but many of them never made it into that lot because of the sheer number of cars carrying all the people who would be attending the funeral. I ended up parking about five or six blocks from the church.

I lost my bearings while walking back up to the church and decided to follow the mass of firefighters lining up in both directions on the street in front of the building. In most cases, a much longer line would have been outside, but there were so many funerals and memorials that morning, each of us had to choose which one to attend. We couldn't all show up in full force for all of them. Still, firefighters lined up in their Class A uniforms with polished shoes, white gloves and tears in their eyes.

I was mustered in rank-and-file without knowing who was on my right or my left. A fresh flow of tears filled my eyes as I stood at attention and saluted the battalion chief's car and the caisson an Engine that had been cleaned and whose hoses had been removed to make room for the casket and the attending pallbearers. You can always tell the difference between an active fire truck and one that is being used for a funeral because, in a funeral, the caisson truck is draped with a black mourning cloth. It is used specifically for firefighters who gave their lives in the line of duty. The FDNY Pipes and Drums used their Scottish bagpipes and drums to play that same death march I had heard too many times before. I thought about how I never wanted to hear that march played again, ever. Yet deep down, I knew all too well that it would be played several more times. In fact, the Emerald Society Pipes and Drums would play that song at about 343 funerals in the two years following the fall of the Twin Towers.

Once the slowly approaching rig was in front of me, I glanced through my tear-filled eyes and saw "Engine 201." I peered again to see if I had misread the number, but the same words, "Engine 201," were still there. Jimmy should have been in a 35 Truck. Even if Ladder 35 had to use an Engine instead of a Ladder, the Engine with which his company shared a firehouse was Engine 40, not Engine 201. I was at the wrong funeral. That wasn't my dear friend Jimmy Giberson in the engine in front of me. How could I have attended the wrong funeral?

I had just about lost it and started to collapse in a blurred, exhausted, dizzy and confused state when the two quick-thinking brothers on either side of me quickly caught me and held me upright. I managed to regain my balance long enough to allow the procession to pass by and continue on to the church. I was just so shaken by the mistake I had made. I couldn't wrap my head around it.

Then I suddenly realized that I wasn't at the wrong funeral. There was no such thing as a wrong funeral because they all were wrong funerals. Not one of those funerals had to happen. I felt myself slowly unraveling and becoming undone. The only way to pull myself together was to take action. Before anyone could ask me if I was ok, I bolted back to my car. I decided that I could still find the right church in time to see my friend Jimmy off. This was my new mission. It was simple enough. But once I made it back to my car, I was shaking so badly that I couldn't put the key in the ignition. Missing Jimmy Giberson's funeral will haunt me the rest of my life. It's already in the rotation of my weird and ugly recurring nightmares.

CHAPTER 8

THE LIVING NIGHTMARE

As powerful and vivid as my nightmares are about missing my friend's funeral, they still pale in comparison to the living nightmare that greeted me once I made it back to Manhattan after leaving the Engine 201 funeral. When I returned to the hotel, Charlie was standing outside with our bags and demanding that we go to the doctor.

"What are you doing?" I asked.

I really wanted to take a shower, but he told me we couldn't go in there.

"What do you mean we can't go in there?"

I knew the room had been paid for, so I didn't understand what he was going on about.

"No, no, no, we gotta leave. You gotta take me to the doctor. I gotta go to the doctor!"

Charlie was ashy and gray as he stood there trembling.

"You didn't go to that firehouse, did you?" I asked, although I was certain that I already knew the answer.

"Yeah!" he said.

"Well, let's go to the firehouse," I replied. If I couldn't shower in the hotel, I knew my old firehouse, "The Pride of Midtown," Engine 54 Ladder 4, would let me shower there.

"No, don't go in the firehouse. Don't go in the firehouse!"

"Charlie, what are you talking about?"

"No, there's a problem, you gotta take me to my cardiologist. I gotta go to the doctor. I called him. You gotta take me to the doctor in Staten Island."

Nothing he was saying at the moment was making sense to me, but the moment he said that he had to see his cardiologist, I wasn't going to argue. Just a year earlier, my brother had undergone open-heart surgery. The surgery had lasted fifteen hours, and the doctors had placed a defibrillator in his chest. He wasn't a well man and I wasn't going to let anything happen to him on my watch. But, while I drove him to see his doctor, I did make him tell me what had happened.

We had come to the city together to participate in a fundraiser for the survivors and family members of those who had lost their lives on September 11th. Although he had always been eccentrically nutty, he was a retired NYC sanitation worker who had never lost his love for his city. He was eager to help, just like everyone else was. At the fundraiser, we had bought about a dozen hats to give away to firefighters. We decided to spend the night in the hotel because I wanted to be back in the city the next day.

Before I had left to attend the funeral, I told Charlie that after he woke up, he should go to a specific diner on Broadway. I knew that the diner served a very inexpensive breakfast. I made it perfectly clear, in no uncertain terms, that he should stay away from the firehouse where he and I had been volunteering for a few days. Having lost fifteen of its firefighters, I knew the house would be inundated with family and friends holding vigil and by distraught firefighters doing their best to continue with their work. He acknowledged my request by repeating what I had told him before he rolled over and went back to sleep. When he got up later and left for breakfast, he took the cell phone and the firefighter shirt with my name on the back, which I had left for him. But he decided to leave behind my advice.

Outside the firehouses were makeshift memorials where people could pin cards, candles, and flowers for the men who had been lost. My old company, "The Pride of Midtown," had lost fifteen guys, probably the most of all the houses. In the meantime, it was still operating, so all kinds of emotions were flying around. My brother started helping the people who were coming by. They would hand him money, cards, and even handwritten notes of gratitude. Charlie would pin up the cards and notes, then put the money in his pocket. He wasn't thinking about putting it in the envelope and bringing it inside. Too much was going on.

When some of the guys came back, one watched Charlie slide the money into his pocket, and the guy's emotions went crazy. Charlie is the type of guy who, when you ask him to go from A to B, goes from A to Z instead. Like I said, he's eccentrically nutty.

The guys put my brother in this house watch and started accusing him of stealing.

"You're stealing money! What are you doing? You're stealing from the widows and orphans! Empty your pockets. Whose money is this?"

Charlie tried to explain, but some of the guys were trying to hit him and rip off his head. Others were stepping up to defend him. They didn't know whether to call the cops or throw him out. Eventually, they just threw him out.

After he told me what had happened, all I could say was, "Didn't I tell you *not* to go to the firehouse? I don't work there, you're wearing my shirt, guys are emotional, and things are going on. I don't work there anymore. You can't just do things like that. Like, maybe if you have a folder and you're putting it in the folder. But you shouldn't be taking any money! I mean, just take the cards. I told you not to be there, there's too much going on. There were widows crying on the freakin' doorstep. I know you were trying to be helpful, everyone knows you were trying to be helpful, but look at what happened!"

By the time we got to the doctor, Charlie was a mess. After they did all they could do for him there at the hospital, he was ordered to go home and rest.

When I went back to my firehouse, they were waiting for me at the door. The anger in their eyes told me that they wanted to kill me before they even said a word.

"We got phone calls from Downtown, Uptown, every firehouse in the city. Every chief is calling and you're a thief," they said. "What are you doing? Why the f**k did you do it?"

They wouldn't let me speak or utter a response. If I stayed any longer, they would have hanged me in the basement, pretended that they found me a week later and called it a suicide.

"No, get the f**k out of here. You're on vacation. Don't go near a f**king firehouse. Don't go near anything. Don't go near Ground Zero."

My current firehouse captain was called up at home while he was on vacation and he didn't want to hear anything. He didn't really know me that well, so his response was a little less than encouraging. He was the one who called me up.

"You stay away," he ordered.

"Yeah, but let me explain…"

"I don't want to hear shit from you! You're a f**king cancer. Get away! Just don't even go near a firehouse."

I was being ostracized. Everyone I knew was in this place and now

I was being cut off from them. First, I'd missed my friend's funeral and now I was being cut off from the rest of the firefighters I knew. I was already mentally and physically exhausted from weeks of alternating between working at Ground Zero and attending funerals for fallen firefighters. But now I was mortified. I was hurt. My brother firefighters thought that I was a thief and a robber of widows and orphans. I was stunned and could barely find words to say.

"Don't call anybody, don't see anybody," they said. "You'll be notified by the IG's office. There will be a full investigation by the police department. Just go home or do us a favor and kill yourself."

No way was this really happening to me. Neither Charlie nor I would do anything as crazy as what I was now being accused of. In fact, none of my brothers would. We simply hadn't been raised that way. We weren't made out of that kind of stuff. I knew that Charlie hadn't come all the way to Manhattan to attend a fundraiser with me just so he could steal money the next day. Charlie and I were the oldest of five siblings and not one of us had lived a life as anything but a public servant.

The only crazy things that Charlie did involved cars. Charlie could do things with vehicles that nobody thought were possible. However, instead of driving for NASCAR, he ended up getting a city job, like my father wanted for all of us, as a driver for the sanitation department. I watched my brother take a garbage truck and drive between the columns and the parked cars on a two-way street without hitting a single one of them. He still hasn't lost his touch and can drive anything. He got married when he was twenty-three or twenty-four to a woman about eight years his junior. His bride's uncle was an electrician and got Charlie into the business for a while. Then Charlie left and became a sanitation worker, like his father-in-law, while the electrician uncle went on to make millions with his business.

My brother Richie was more of a quiet kid. He was about a year-

and-a-half to two years younger than I was. I remember him carrying around a Huckleberry Hound stuffed animal. When he was five years old, he wore shorts with button-down shirts and bow ties while he carried around Huckleberry Hound. I don't know why he wanted to wear the bow tie. All I know is that my mother would have to bow tie him when we went to church or to Grandma's house. He just liked the bow tie. For a couple of years, that was how he dressed. My mother still has pictures of him wearing these bow ties.

Richie stayed in college until he took a summer job as a postman. He never returned to college. He's still a postman today in New Jersey—not a city employee like our father wanted, but Dad wasn't disappointed that Richie became a federal employee. He had been a postman for about thirty-six years. He always had a great route. People have given him their old cars. He's just that kind of guy. They make him lunch. They love him. He's the best. He always took care of people. "I'll take care of that. I'll straighten it out. I'll replace your light bulb or the batteries in your smoke detector." Whatever trivial thing he could do for somebody who had no family, he did. He did the buildings on Ocean Parkway in Brooklyn, and he had a great route. He also had a good Christmas route. The people loved him. Richie didn't want to transfer to Jersey when he moved there, but now his route is located in a senior development neighborhood and they all love him.

And what's not to love? He's great and he has a side business washing, repairing and installing window screens. He hires his two sons, Chris and Matt, to help him with the bull work and hires his daughter, Jessica, for moral support and to share time and stories with the clients. Almost all the proceeds go into his kids' pockets. Richie takes one hundred dollars for the supplies, a little bit for gas money and fifty dollars for himself. The rest he gives to his kids.

He married the girl who lived up the street from our childhood home, put his kids through college and then got divorced. He still manages to be friends with his ex-wife. He's the quintessential best father in the world. He takes care of his kids' cars, and he handles all the stuff that teenagers neglect to do or set aside. He's a good guy. He's a really good guy. He doesn't chase women. He loves the Green Bay Packers, the Baltimore Orioles, the Boston Bruins (go figure), and fantasy sports but he is really all about anything and everything involving his kids. That's all he does. He chases his kids to this day, and they're college graduates.

His two boys, Christopher and Matthew, should be very proud of their dad for the sacrifices he made on their behalf. His only daughter, Jessica, after finishing school, got a great job in the medical field. All he said was, "Make sure you stay on top of this and make sure you get that done," and he paid for everything. He remarried in late September 2013 to a wonderful gal who happened to be his first love. It was his Kismet. Richie's a great guy and it's time for him to share and enjoy a wonderful life with his loving bride Linda and his new family: the lovely ten-year-old twins Jessica and Corrine.

Craig joined the Marines and came back a different guy. He was a passive guy when he left but returned with the mind of a killer. He served in Iraq and Kuwait for a year following the September 11th attacks. As soon as he got out, he got a job as a bartender for a catering hall. He met his wife there and they got married in one of the top catering and special event venues in New York, called Russo's on the Bay in Howard Beach. They had worked there for a couple of years when it first opened; the owner wanted them to get married there and gave them a great deal. Craig wore his Marine dress blues and several of his fellow Marines were there with him. His wife made an entrance up through the floor of the hall. It was amazing!

They had children, a boy and girl. Just like Richie did, Craig made sure that his kids got everything they wanted and everything he thought they should want. Unfortunately, like Richie, he also ended up divorced. His divorce was for a very different reason, however. One day when Craig was in line at the airport with his wife, he told her that he was going to turn around and snap the neck of one of the guys behind them in line. Then he was going to grab a second guy's leg and cut his throat. Craig's wife was so afraid of him, she sought a divorce. He had never laid a hand on her. He had never assaulted her. But she just didn't feel safe around him anymore.

He went to see doctors, who diagnosed him with Post-Traumatic Stress Disorder (PTSD). He was really quiet about it and none of us knew anything about it until this happened. By the time he'd come back, I was already married and starting a family, so I wasn't overly involved in his personal affairs. He had always been a good man, but the war changed him.

Our younger brother Greg also became a sanitation worker— another public servant.

At the end of the investigation, the conclusion was that the allegations were unfounded. I was exonerated and indemnified by the city and all the powers that be, and I was allowed to keep my job. Unfortunately, it didn't matter one iota that the investigation had found me innocent. By the time the report was released, the story had spread throughout the FDNY. Everyone thought of me as a scumbag thief. You would have thought I had robbed three banks and murdered six people, then run over Mother Teresa during the getaway. It didn't matter what the investigation had uncovered or what I said. When I walked down the street and firefighters recognized me, they would spit on me and call me a scumbag. No one wanted to talk to me.

"Don't even come near me. I don't even want to see you."

I got emotional because these weren't complete strangers who were upset with me. These were my friends who didn't want to talk to me.

I had done some crazy things during my years as a firefighter, but none of them had ever elicited this kind of response. I remember getting a phone call at 9:00 a.m. after a long night of drinking and partying. I scrambled around as the phone rang, almost falling off the bed. Finally, I rolled around and grabbed the phone.

"This is Captain Grasso. Why aren't you at work today?"

I was sleeping, so I rubbed my eyes, thinking it was a prank. "Are you shitting me? I'm off today. I'm not working today."

"No, Ron, I'm not shitting you!"

All of a sudden, I went from zero to one hundred. I was supposed to be at work already, so all I could say was, "I'll be right there!" I don't even think he had time to tell me, "Take your time." He was that kind of guy When he knew someone was coming, he'd leave space in the book for them. But he would never tell me that because I was a *probie*!

In red, he'd write down when you'd gotten there because everything was down to the minute. Firefighter Parker, RFD (ready for duty) at 7:59, or Firefighter Smith, RFD, 8:01.

If someone didn't show up, he'd always leave a space. Then he'd talk to the officer, or he'd call the guy up before you. However, I didn't get a phone call from any of these jerks because they probably didn't even know who I was.

I guess they knew I was supposed to come in because there was a line-up. You know who's coming, you cross them off the list, this day you got relieved, whatever, Carroll for Smith or Parker for Sollicito.

At the time, I had a brand-new souped-up 1983 Pontiac Trans Am Indy Pace Car that my girlfriend had gotten from California. I drove through the Brooklyn Battery Tunnel when they were changing the lights from green to yellow to red. You know they're going to switch the sides, and there had been a little bit of traffic going in the tunnel.

I drove through the tunnel the wrong way. I watched it go from green to red. That means they're going to open up the other side for people to drive in. But I did it in the same tunnel, so I was able to cross over if necessary. I didn't choose to go in a different tunnel because if I had gotten stuck, I'd be screwed.

I think I made it to Ladder 4 Manhattan in about fourteen minutes that day. When I arrived, the captain raised his eyebrows and gave me a look of surprise that seemed to say, "You're here? Didn't I tell you to take your time?"

It was one of those days. And although it was unheard of for an FDNY firefighter to sleep through his shift, the incident was shaken off and merely dismissed (although I did polish a lot of brass that week). There was no drama behind it.

The other unflattering way I ran into the captain was the time when I drove my motorcycle into Manhattan from Brooklyn. I remember trying to figure out the best route to take. With a motorcycle, I could save time by squeezing through traffic. I was between 3rd and Lexington heading west on 42nd Street. I was in the right lane and preparing to make a right turn. There was a red light, but that wouldn't stop me from making my turn. A truck was in front of me and a cabbie came up from the left side. He was coming all the way over with bad intentions. I watched the driver weave through traffic, but he never looked at me. He didn't even notice me as he swerved at a high rate of speed into the turning lane where I was located. He pushed me out of the lane.

I was nudged into the high curb and pushed onto the sidewalk, where I dropped my bike. He didn't hit me hard, as he forcefully braked and knocked me over. I could feel the blood rushing into my face and throbbing as the self-righteous anger of a young man grew in me. I was going three miles an hour and I let every cuss word fly out of my mouth in every possible combination I could think of.

I used to carry my spare helmet under my elbow, like an elbow pad. It was a shortie helmet, so I would wear my helmet and carry the other one because I didn't have a place to put it. I remember screaming at this guy, who was looking at me with an expression that seemed to say, "I don't know." He hadn't seen anything, and I was still upset about my bike being pushed to the ground and scratched. Through the window, I gave him a little shove with my spare helmet to release him from his zombie stare.

The next thing I knew, he had grabbed me. Then I grabbed him. We started pulling at each other through the cab window. When I heard the sirens of the quickly approaching cops, I really got upset because I had to get to work. I didn't have time for any of this crap. So, I just jumped on the motorcycle and rode off toward my firehouse on 48th and 8th. I was about a half mile away on 42nd and I still had to deal with traffic.

When I finally got to the firehouse, I pulled into the little courtyard where the firefighters could each put one car. Alternately, guys parked their bicycles (or, in my case, my motorcycle) there. It was the same courtyard to which the senior firefighters had sent me to check on the barbecue only to then douse me with water. I put my bike there and then went into the house. I was basically on time, but I still had to go upstairs for a quick-change. When I went back downstairs, I saw two detectives. I knew they were looking for me.

One of them looked up at me and said, "You left the scene of an accident and you beat up this cab driver."

For the second time that morning, I felt my heart pounding and all the blood rushing to my head, but I tried to play it cool. "Yeah, I had some kind of altercation with some asshole cab driver, you know?" My demeanor didn't change their minds. They put me in their unmarked police car and took me down to their precinct so I could tell them what happened. I told them that the guy had landed both me and my bike on the ground, but all I heard back was, "Yeah, but he's all beat up." Oh my God! Well, somebody had to win! The whole situation annoyed me and I wasn't afraid to show it. I finally looked at one of the cops and tried to level with him. "Hey, I've got to work. What are you doing? Someone who just worked a fifteen-hour shift is working overtime to cover my assignment until I get back."

Before I knew it, the rig from my firehouse was outside the police station to pick me up. The captain was in there. He walked in and laid into the first person he saw. "Hey, listen, I followed the cop car. What are you jerks doing?"

They started explaining the situation to my captain but he didn't let up. "Is this guy in the hospital?"

I hadn't put him in the hospital. I had only roughed him up a bit. By the end of the conversation, we learned that a lady had been in the back of the cab and she had no idea that the cab driver had knocked me over. She thought I had just attacked this guy through the window for no reason, so she called the cops.

When Captain Grasso heard that the cab driver wanted to press charges, he started asking more questions. He found out from the detectives that the cab driver had a driving record that unfolded like Bullwinkle's calling card. He also had a suspended driver's license. This made it easier for them to believe that he had run me off the road. My captain reassured them that if they didn't lynch me at high noon, he would discipline me himself. No one cared about the damage to my bike because I didn't have a scratch on me. The other guy looked a little worse for the wear, and the detectives kept bringing up the fact that I had left the scene before they arrived.

You can imagine how they felt when I decided to simply walk out of the station so I could get back to work. I knew that I hadn't murdered the guy or done any serious, permanent damage. This was unnecessary drama that was keeping me from doing what I had to do. Once I got outside, I saw the rig and all I could do was sigh. After about six months as a *probie* firefighter, this was how I finally met the captain. When I got back to the firehouse, a senior guy with about thirty years on the job walked up, looked down at me, and said, "So, we got a criminal working with us, huh?" I remember feeling a little nervous about how the firefighters were going to take it, but next he said, "Get to work," and the other guys started clapping like it was a joke. Instead of ostracizing me for ending up in a police precinct, my captain defended me and everyone treated it like a joke instead of ostracizing me. However, the captain did keep his word to the police officers: he made me do all the house watch duty and spiff up more of the truck's brass hardware.

Yet even I had to admit that my current situation was different from the others. Now we all were mentally and physically drained while struggling each day to help rebuild a city that had been destroyed by people we didn't know—people who had attacked us for reasons none of us understood. At the time, a nameless and faceless villain was out there—one who had brought all this on us. So, when allegations arose about a theft committed by someone who could be identified, the distraught firefighters finally had a scapegoat they could punish. I never signed up to play that role, but I guess someone had to sooner or later.

I was smart enough to leave their presence. As the days passed and the anger didn't, I didn't know what to do. I had to reach out to somebody who would listen to me and hear me out. I had few options. I didn't want to go upstairs with this, although there was a chief who knew me pretty well. He was well-respected downtown and he used to be my lieutenant in that Manhattan firehouse consisting of Engine 54, Ladder 4 and Battalion 9. He had led me in some of the most rip-roaring tenement fires, teaching me many great skills as he operated flawlessly with jackrabbit speed and agility. Joe was a nice guy, a really good, decent, fair guy. He was smart—a superbly gifted firefighter and officer. He had the big office. I want to say he was among the top twenty to twenty-five chiefs in the FDNY. Reluctantly, and with my tail between my legs, I went downtown to see him.

"Chief, I swear, this is exactly what happened."

"Well, I understand…" he said.

It turned out that he knew my current captain well.

"You know, I'll call your captain and see."

He actually called him right then and there, but the captain didn't want to talk to him. Here was a chief respectfully calling a lower ranking captain and the captain's response was that he didn't want to hear it. He was on vacation and that was that. Not a real class act.

The chief told me to go home, that this thing would pass. But it wasn't passing! So, I went back to the firehouse, where the guys still wanted to kill me. I mean, the guys didn't want to talk to me. No charges were ever filed against me because the investigation had shown that I wasn't there and that Charlie hadn't actually taken the money, but no one wanted to hear that. It didn't matter. Eventually, I decided that the best thing to do was to volunteer for the details no one else wanted so I could still work but be away from everyone. Nobody wants to go to *The Pile*, so I'll go to *The Pile*. I'll take this detail, not a problem.

I took the detail and went right back into Ground Zero. I worked through the end of Thanksgiving. I worked through Christmas. I worked through New Year's Eve. On New Year's Day, I actually found a brother firefighter from Brooklyn's 201 Engine—the same company as that of the firefighter whose funeral I had accidentally attended months earlier.

I jumped into a hole, found a coat and started digging. The firefighter was upside down so I lay backward because our bunker gear included boots, pants, heavy-duty suspenders, and a coat that forms one unit, ensuring that everything stays intact. I soon realized that there was no helmet, no head. I jumped into the hole and tried to get him. It was unbelievable. As I dug him out, I realized that I knew the hero firefighter. He was Christopher Pickford of Engine Company 201—another Brooklyn brother. I sought to get him out as carefully and with as much respect as was humanly possible. I wrapped him in the flag and gently placed him in the Stokes basket. Just as we had done for every person recovered from the site, we stopped everything and shut the site down to carry our brother, Christopher Pickford, out of the bowels of that hellhole pit. All the brothers and workers silently lined up and saluted farewell to a true hero. I think we found a total of six people that New Year's Day. The closure was good for the grieving families.

That was one of the last details I served in Brooklyn. The tension in the Staten Island firehouse was so bad, I tried to transfer, but no one would do me any favors by allowing me to transfer into their firehouse. I was stuck to rot there for the rest of my career.

To this day, many guys won't talk to me. They just don't care. I don't know. And everybody else just went, "Oh, we made a mistake. Ok." Honestly, I think of all the guys who ostracized me, only one lieutenant—who was a class act—apologized to me.

"I'm sorry."

"Thanks a lot. It means a lot to me."

Not that I thought the whole company would apologize; they were a bunch of deadbeats being controlled by a few bullies. To be honest, they worked on the very end of Staten Island and didn't really want to put out any fires. They weren't that kind of gung-ho company. Among them was a construction worker who owned a big business and who seemed to regard the fire department as his part-time job. It seemed like the firehouse was where they came to sleep. I don't know. I had never worked in a company like that. Not to put down Staten Island companies —not at all, as most of the men who work in the firehouses of Staten Island are brave and dedicated to their profession. They do a fair amount of fire duty on the island's north shore and in other, overpopulated, run-down neighborhoods. But this was certainly not the career I had in mind when I had become a *probie* so many years earlier.

It had become apparent that the time for my retirement was on the horizon. I shunned the thought many times, but it inevitably kept popping up in my head. I often asked myself whether I was considering retirement on my own terms or on someone else's terms. Over the years, I learned that passing the torch of the New York City Fire Department was recognized as being just as important as taking your first steps into *Probie School.* The perfect balance of learning, communicating, and teaching was required to pass the torch.

This final phase has been acknowledged by many as one of the most difficult, indelible and intricate decisions that a New York City firefighter will make. Some firefighters have that decision stolen from them due to injuries they incur on the job. Still others have made their last fateful steps precariously into a literal blaze of glory.

I spent the last few months before my May 12, 2004 retirement alone in a quiet and tranquil bubble. The time passed slowly—painfully slow. On my last day, I finally emptied my locker, barely looking at or reminiscing about its contents as I had done in the past when moving my items from one house to another. In times past, I would always come across something that I'd forgotten. The rediscovery would bring about a good chuckle and make me smile, but not this time. This wasn't a time for reminiscing because part of my reason for leaving was to forget.

Knowing that I was doing this for the very last time, I finished cleaning out my locker in record time. I packed my gear and quietly left. Hardly anyone said goodbye. It was as if a ghost was leaving. I knew that I had accomplished all I could as a New York City firefighter, so a calm, rewarding solace and peace embraced me as I left the quarters of Engine 164 and Ladder 84, the house known as "Close to the Edge."

The smiles on their faces told me that Judy and my kids were happy with my newfound freedom at home. I was also happy to be able to spend more time with them. I smiled more often. However, mentally, I was still a train wreck about having been relieved of my duties as a firefighter. It was beginning to destroy the man I was. I became more distraught, angry and confused. I began to question things that I couldn't go back and change.

I spent most of my time at home, alone. For the first time in my life, I became a recluse. I avoided people at all costs. I wasn't comfortable around anyone other than my immediate family. A great deal of time passed, and I let the distance between me and my friends grow. I hardly spoke to any of them. When we did speak, I was uninterested, brief and curt over the phone. The days of getting together with friends for club hockey, golf and softball games became a distant memory. I simply had no interest, feeling the way I did when I was still the man I knew and recognized—when I was still a loved and respected firefighter.

CHAPTER 9

CREATIVE RELEASE

It was one of those bitterly cold winter nights. Not much was happening in our battalion, which was unusual, considering the cold. We should have known that it wouldn't be that way for long.

Teddy was a fearless firefighter on duty at one of our own battalion's firehouses on Manhattan's West Side—Engine 40, Ladder 35 on 66th Street and Amsterdam Avenue. Unbeknownst to the sleeping city, this fearless firefighter doubled as an off-duty recluse and drunk. And now that Jekyll was off duty, he had transformed into Hyde for the sleepy evening. The rapidly approaching date of a divorce he didn't want had inspired a steady pace of all-night binge drinking in an attempt to drown his sorrows. After failing to find a resolution at the bottom of several empty glasses, he left the bar to wander alone and dazed around the west side of the city.

Lost in his slurred thoughts about the divorce, Teddy failed to notice the uneven sidewalk. He stumbled and fell into the glass window of a twenty-four-hour doughnut shop. Fortunately, there was no damage to the glass. However, two of New York City's finest happened to be sitting on the opposite side of the shop's glass window. The startling crash prompted one officer to squeeze his jelly doughnut hard enough that it squirted all over his uniform. The other officer spilled his hot coffee in his lap.

The coffee-drenched officer immediately reached for his glass of ice water and doused his lap to relieve the excruciating pain that the piping-hot liquid had created. Teddy watched the entire chain of events and instantly unleashed his signature laugh and howl. He laughed so uncontrollably that he emptied his bladder and bowels onto the front and back of his own pants. Yet even this self-degrading display wasn't enough to appease the officers and allow Teddy to escape their crosshairs.

The cop covered in jelly doughnut was Officer Muldoon. He was a hard-nosed, no-nonsense, tough, jelly-doughnut-loving cop who demanded respect. Teddy's unbridled laughter infuriated the officer, who now sought revenge. His partner had an interesting reputation of his own. The coffee-drenched officer was the notorious Bend-a-Cop Sullivan, who had earned his nickname by repeatedly writing summonses to fellow off-duty police officers and their families. On this night, he wasn't after any other cops. He was after the man who had caused his favorite evening coffee to scorch his lap.

Out the door they came, as furious and ravenous as any human can possibly be. They were way past angry. The steam coming out of their noses as they forcefully exhaled into the cold night air was so intense, it appeared as if the fire of a jet engine was embedded within the exhaust of their breath. A trail of steam even radiated from Officer Sullivan's lap as he moved. And Muldoon's uniform resembled a cinematic depiction of a bloodstained, shot-down gunslinger in a Sam Peckinpah Western, using jelly to imitate blood. The intense look on their faces suggested that this wasn't a laughing matter. Yet Teddy and the two night-shift workers in the doughnut shop still managed to appreciate the humor of the spectacle and could hardly contain themselves.

The officers reached Teddy in exactly the same place where they first laid eyes on him. He was now rolling on the pavement, still uncontrollably laughing.

"So, you think you're funny, do ya? I'll show you what's funny," said the giant-sized Muldoon in his Irish brogue as he towered over Teddy.

Muldoon quickly grabbed Teddy by the collar and lifted him off the ground just in time for Sullivan to let loose with a quick punch to Teddy's gut. The blow triggered a fresh release of feces and urine, which leaked through Teddy's trousers and embedded a new smell into the already jelly-stained uniform that Muldoon wore.

"What the hell are you doing?" Teddy chimed in. "It's me, Teddy, your brother-in-law!"

Muldoon quickly dropped Teddy back to the ground in a heap as he focused his angry, blood-red eyes long enough to recognize his kinfolk. Teddy leaned over onto his side and quickly fell asleep. He was completely oblivious to the mess he was in and the fact that he was lying outside on a sidewalk.

"He's a firefighter. We best drop him off at his firehouse where he'll do no more harm. We'll let those crony old hosebags babysit him. It's only a few blocks from here."

They procured a body bag from the trunk of the squad car and carefully placed it in the back seat before loading Teddy into the cruiser to prevent further damage. Cleaning a uniform was one thing but having to clean the cloth bucket seats of the squad car in which they spent their entire shift was another.

After they hit a series of potholes, Teddy momentarily awoke from his stupor to find himself wrapped in the all-too-familiar body bag, bouncing around in the backseat of a car.

"Let me out!" he screamed at the top of his lungs.

Teddy knew that Muldoon's family had an extremely dark side; he thought he was going to be "deep-sixed" in the Hudson River by the cop whose sister he had married. Teddy had never spoken to anyone about the dark side of the Muldoon family. Not even to Father Mulligan at St. Patrick's Cathedral, with whom he occasionally shared a pint or two. Not even at Holy Confession was this ever uttered.

Although Teddy knew that his in-laws were active members of The Westies, the infamously crazy and deadly street gang that even the Italian Mafia feared, he hadn't learned this until after he had fallen in love and proposed. At that point, he didn't have many options. He couldn't break his fiancée's heart by calling off the engagement and expect to live through the end of the day. Teddy was stuck—or at least he was until the issue of divorce started coming up more often in conversations with his wife.

The Westies' domain was Hell's Kitchen on Manhattan's West Side, from the Midtown Tunnel on the south side up to Central Park. The Irish immigrant neighborhood gang wasn't all that large in numbers considering the amount of crime, murder and havoc they wreaked. Mostly devoid of formal education, they instead had street smarts. They all had master's degrees in robbery, kidnapping, arson, killing, dismembering, lying and cheating. And they all had doctorates in drinking.

They were also skilled with their hands, knives, guns and anything else they could get their hands on. They had been known to chop off their adversaries' hands, store them in freezers, and use the fingerprints on guns and knives to cover their tracks. I'm sure if you Googled "psychopaths," you'd find them on the top of the list. They could do a person bodily harm without blinking an eye and with no remorse. What would appear to be a friendly conversation may become deadly in a nanosecond. Sometimes a person became an adversary simply because they didn't like his face.

You wouldn't have wanted to be in any of the Westside local bars in Hell's Kitchen. You wouldn't even have wanted to glance at or make eye contact with any of them; otherwise, they might have killed you just for fun. It all depended on their moods. Upon entering any one of these watering holes, you would be eyeballed up and down within seconds. If you didn't pass the eyeball test and were unfortunate enough to not have Spidey Senses or any inert ability to realize you were in the Devil's Lair, you may have made the deadly mistake of taking an unwelcomed seat at the bar where they held court. To have them physically kick you out the door while rifling through your pockets would be a blessing. The alternative might have been to separate your hand from your body so that they would have a new set of fingerprints.

Inspired by the mostly vacant and unused waterfront just a few blocks west of their location, Sullivan and Muldoon briefly discussed introducing the maligned and stinky Teddy to the Hudson. They had already wrapped him inside the body bag; it wouldn't be difficult for each of them to grab an end of the bag and send Teddy on a watery journey. Sullivan made a quick right turn and headed to the Westside piers.

All appeared quiet on the waterfront. Not a soul was in sight and even street lamps were broken. It was too bitterly cold for the usual bums, vagrants, and transsexual hookers to be out on that brutal night. They only things they found were a couple of dead, frozen wharf rats. I don't know how close they really came to deep-sixing Teddy. They would have had to chop and break the ice in the Hudson just to get the body in the water. That was too much work and they didn't have the proper tools. Sullivan said they could've used their six-shooters, but they'd have had to explain where the bullets went and it might have made too much noise.

As Teddy heard the gist of the conversation between the two flatfoots, he began to flail about in an effort to escape.

"You'll never get away with this!" Teddy slurred in defiance from the backseat.

Fortunately for Teddy, the consensus was to drop him off at his firehouse on Amsterdam and 66th Street, letting the firefighters deal with the drunken mess that belonged to them.

By the time the car came to a stop, Teddy's senses were awake enough to let him know that he was in a safe and familiar setting. He was back at the quarters of Engine 40, Ladder 35—home of the "Cavemen." As they pulled up to the apron of the firehouse, Sullivan hit a few of the trash cans that had been set out that evening. The action only served to disturb the one-eyed firehouse cat, affectionately known as Blinky, who was distracted from his meal of Chinese food, lasagna, pizza, chili, tomato soup and borscht, all of which had been freshly deposited a short time earlier. However, when house watchman O'Donovan heard the noise outside the firehouse at 4:15 a.m., he prepared for action.

It wasn't unusual for victims of muggings or rapes to arrive at the firehouse door for assistance. Unsure whether he would be meeting both the victim and the attacker, O'Donovan armed himself with a baseball bat and opened the door to greet the source of the noise. As he stepped just outside the doorway, he saw Teddy in his distressed state, a big smile on his face while Muldoon and Sullivan cursed Teddy on their way back to the cop car. Teddy clutched the side of a trash can with one hand to help him get back on his feet. The other hand clutched Muldoon's cigarettes, which he had deftly lifted from his oblivious brother-in-law while bumping into Muldoon after he got out of the car.

Teddy stumbled past the bewildered O'Donovan, who had holstered the forty-four-ounce Louisville Slugger in its custom-built rack on the side of the house watch wall. The house watchman shook his head as he retreated to his desk and tried to count the number of times he had seen Teddy on such a familiar bender after a crazy night out. He sighed as he debated whether to report Teddy's condition to the firehouse officers in the hopes that they might force him to go into rehab for his own good.

Teddy somehow managed to liberate his alcohol-abused body from his fouled clothing while walking, crawling, and pulling himself up the steps to the firehouse recreation room. By the time he reached the couch, he was wearing only his raccoon skin hat while still clutching his newly acquired cigarettes. Teddy decided to rest on the couch for a while before heading off to the showers. He conveniently found the matches on the coffee table in front of him and lit up a cigarette just before he turned on the TV. Teddy dozed off only seconds after lighting the fateful butt.

Downstairs, the banging was much fiercer than the sound O'Donovan had heard upon Teddy's arrival. Once again, O'Donovan opened the door armed with the Slugger. Two NYC sanitation workers were there to report a fire that was erupting out the window of an adjoining building on the 66th Street side of the block. Yet as Danny stepped outside to take a look, he noticed that the other building wasn't on fire. His own firehouse was the one hosting the roaring flames.

O'Donovan quickly ran inside the firehouse and tapped three bells before urgently, yet professionally, summoning both the Engine and the Truck companies over the house intercom. At the sound of the bells, the brothers in the house quickly began grabbing their gear to respond. When O'Donovan announced that the 1075 code for working fire was referencing a blaze in their own firehouse, some of the groggy brothers thought they'd misheard what O'Donovan had said. Others were confused because they hadn't heard the usual *bee-boop* sound from the teleprinter that always preceded the ringing of the bells and the intercom announcement before a run. Still others said nothing even though they smelled smoke; they thought it was a lingering smell from someone's gear after the last run.

O'Donovan repeated the announcement again and again while climbing into his own gear. Thank God the Engine captain was working that night, as was a senior lieutenant in the Truck. The captain realized the severity of the problem and quickly asked O'Donovan if he had reported the fire to dispatch.

"I didn't think you would have wanted me to do that, Captain."

The Engine 40 captain sighed in relief that no one had been notified; he gave a slight nod that let O'Donovan know he had made the right decision. It was bad enough to have a fire in the firehouse—they didn't need to let everyone else know about it. The Engine Company stretched the hose line up the interior steps of the firehouse toward the recreation room, which seemed to be the origin of the flames. The Engine's chauffeur left the lights and sirens off as he pulled the Engine a few feet out from the firehouse, lining it up with the fire hydrant. He quickly hooked up the hose to the hydrant.

The Truck also pulled out of the firehouse without lights or sirens to make a right turn up 66th Street. The OV and *roof man* grabbed a 35-foot extension ladder and quickly made their way to the roof, which they vented by opening the bulkhead door. This created a place for the fire to vent once the hose was turned on. They also quickly looked over all four sides of the roof before reporting over the radio to the lieutenant that the roof was open, and no victims were outside any of the building's perimeters. The lieutenant and forcible entry team of 35 Truck grabbed their hand tools and donned their masks before joining Engine 40, which was flanking out its line up the steps in preparation for a battle with the flames.

They knew the layout of their own home all too well, and there were no doors to force open in search of flames or trapped victims. They just needed to thoroughly search for any firefighters in distress because of the fire. A little venting for the flames and all should be well. The room was fully *involved* with fire by the time they reached it with the hose line. Engine 40's captain gave the order over the radio to "start water" and the Engine 40 chauffeur reported back a second later that it was on the way.

Engine 40 stretched an inch-and-three-quarter line quickly and steadily in the aggressive interior attack of the fire. Ladder 35's *iron man*, who carried tools to force open doors or remove large obstacles preventing a safe exit, gave a preliminary report to the Truck lieutenant that the initial search was negative. Soon, this was followed by the same response from the *can man*, who always entered fires with a small fire extinguisher to knock down fires on his way toward finding victims. The officer of 35 Truck also reported that no one was in the sitting room and that a secondary search was underway.

Engine 40's *nozzle man* and his backup, who secured and maneuvered the rest of the hose line, did a superb job knocking down the fire in just a few minutes. Once the last of the flames had been extinguished, the firefighters started wondering out loud how the fire had started.

"Maybe it was electrical," offered one firefighter.

It could have been an electrical issue or overloaded circuits. Each of them wondered why no one knew the answer to what would become their firehouse's dark and embarrassing secret. Then, O'Donovan remembered Teddy's arrival shortly before the whole episode began. Where was that drunken fool? O'Donovan used his handie-talkie to report that Teddy was in the quarters and that everyone was to look for him. He guessed that Teddy might know how this disaster had begun.

It turned out that at the time Teddy lit his cigarette on the couch, Tripod, the three-legged firehouse dog, paid the drunk a friendly visit, cuddling with Teddy on the couch. Tripod probably liked all the funky and unusual smells emanating from Teddy. When the couch erupted into flames, the poor pooch's good rear leg was burned. Tripod bit the slumbering Teddy several times to wake him before they retreated to the bathroom.

Now that he had finally made it into the bathroom, Teddy turned on the shower faucet only to fall asleep beneath the steady flow of water. He was totally unfazed by what was occurring all around him. Tripod stayed faithfully by his side.

The Truck search team found Teddy in the shower a few minutes after O'Donovan's tip. Upon their less-than-silent arrival, Teddy awoke, saw the men in full gear, and asked his brother firefighters if the captain had them drilling in the middle of the night. Although they didn't yet know the full story, the lingering smell of urine, feces, and alcohol told them what they needed to know. They left Teddy in the shower, the water still running, while they tended to Tripod's burnt rear leg.

Miraculously, the city of two million Manhattanites remained unaware of the fiasco that had just taken place in one of their firehouses despite the half dozen national TV broadcasting offices, newspapers, and media centers located within a few blocks of the firehouse. Only the two NYC sanitation workers who had reported the flames to O'Donovan knew that there had been a fire that bitter night. Their discretion earned them a lifetime supply of fresh, hot coffee, bagels, and (don't tell Muldoon) jelly donuts any time they passed the firehouse on their allotted breaks.

The following day, the 9th Battalion chief showed up for his daily rounds. As usual, the chief's car was parked on the apron of the firehouse. His aide, Harris, a salty twenty-nine-year veteran, strolled in with Chief Rooney, one of the most respected chiefs in the fire department. His time on the job eclipsed Harris's by over a decade. His invaluable knowledge had been utilized many times throughout his career.

Upon the chief's entrance into the *quarters*, the *probie* sitting on house watch duty announced: "Battalion 9 chief in quarters," which prompted an immediate lining up of all the officers and members for roll call. Harris exchanged the inter-office mailbag with the *probie* on the watch as he turned and asked the senior man and Engine 40 chauffeur, Allen Fineberg, if he had missed a job the previous night. Allen simply shrugged in response.

The chief dismissed the men after roll call and continued up the stairs to the officer's office. Followed by the captain of 40 Engine and by the lieutenant of 35 Truck, the chief stopped at the top of the stairs, then quickly turned around to descend. On his way down, he growled, "I don't know how you jokers pulled it off, but I'm coming back for a full house inspection in a week. By then, all of this will have been a mirage." He put on his chief's hat and entered the 9th Battalion GMC Suburban. Harris, his aide, and driver slowly pulled away from the firehouse. Not a word was uttered as they drove off.

"And that's the 'Teddy the Firebug' story that I've been writing," I proudly announced as I neatly stacked and set aside all the papers containing the story. looked up at my psychiatrist, Dr. Charles Carluccio, for a response.

I had started seeing Dr. Carluccio at the recommendation of my friend and neighbor, Mike Kevlin. Mike had been my neighbor while I was still living in New Jersey. We were close friends due to our kids and our friendly neighborhood. My son Blaze and Mike's son Michael were in the same class at school. It wasn't long before Mike and I started to recognize each other at the boys' sporting events, while walking our dogs around the neighborhood, at the grocery store, or even just driving through the area.

An interesting note about Mike is that he had a lot of personal connections to the World Trade Center. He has an amazing, ironic story.

At age seventeen, Mike became a United States Marine during the Vietnam War. It was probably around 1966 or 1967. He went overseas and landed in the middle of the night.

"Corporal Kevlin," they told him, "take this jeep with a canon on the back of it about ten to twelve miles away by yourself at night with no lights on. Welcome to Vietnam, son!"

He was definitely on the cusp of enemy territory when he left this camp. It wasn't like he was on a highway. He was definitely in danger and he was by himself. However, he had an order and a jeep and that was that. He completed his task.

Mike had been trained in the Marines. He had a passion for radios and had been a ham radio operator as a kid. He used to go to Radio Row quite often to buy all the components, parts, radio antennas, enhancers and transistors. A lot of stores in that area sold this type of equipment and he could buy it for relatively cheap because it was all surplus military stuff from World War II and Korea.

Now, as a Marine, he had just arrived and received the latest training from the US Marine Corps to operate its radios for aerial bombardments, mortar placement, ships, and guns, as well as to communicate with the troops on the ground. If a convoy went out, Mike's jeep was in the middle of the convoy and protected to the utmost because it had top-secret state-of-the-art radio technology. It wasn't just the standard day-to-day walkie-talkie. Mike was the liaison who communicates commands and reports both to and from battleships and ground troops. He knew how to operate all of it. That's why he was made a corporal and given his own jeep, with his own name on it.

Mike will never fly in a plane, though. If I told him that I'd send him a first-class ticket to visit me, he would drive. During one of his deployments in Vietnam, he got on a small plane that crashed and split in half upon landing. He found himself tumbling out of the back of the plane. In the military, he had to get on a plane a couple of times afterward so that he could get back home, but he'll never get on a plane again. It's another ironic thing that he survived this plane crash and survived the later plane crashes on September 11th that killed more than 2,000 people.

Both Mike's father and grandfather were ironworkers who built bridges, tunnels, buildings, so when Mike came out of Vietnam, he became an ironworker. It was the nepotism thing. He was Irish and almost all the kids in his neighborhood were ironworkers. He worked on buildings in downtown Manhattan and he had watched the construction of the World Trade Center while he was on his work site. In addition, he had done some work on the World Trade Center during periods when extra guys were needed to finish the job.

Next, Mike became a Port Authority cop. Now he was working inside the building that he'd helped build as a Port Authority sergeant.

His story is pretty amazing in terms of how it keeps tying back to that area—first when it was Radio Row, then he was part of the crew that helped build the World Trade Center, and finally when he was a Port Authority sergeant who was in that building every single day before he returned to New Jersey to sign out. It's also ironic that Mike was deathly afraid of planes after the crash that he survived, and that he then survived the crash that destroyed the building and the area where he had hung out as a child—the same building that he had helped build, and the building where he worked. If he had stayed on that job another eight or nine months, that plane would have killed him, even though after Vietnam he had vowed to never get inside a plane again.

Mike knew many of the Port Authority police officers who had been killed there, so in many ways, he understood what I was going through a little better than did any of my other non-firefighter friends. Because he lived so close to me, he probably noticed that I was often down in the dumps, that I just wasn't the fun-loving guy I normally was. I don't know if he ever noticed that I stopped doing things around the house like taking out the garbage pails. I don't know if he noticed that I walked and talked to myself around the cul-de-sac where I lived. Maybe he caught a glimpse of me stumbling or bumbling after I had been drinking. Then again, maybe it was just his cop instincts that told him I needed to talk to someone.

Whatever the reason, he did a little asking around and got me the contact information for Dr. Carluccio.

"This is the guy whom guys use when they have a problem. He's great and he's a local."

At first, I was forced to see the psychiatrist. Everyone else wanted me to see him, but I wasn't on that ship. I was disenchanted and disconnected from nearly everyone around me. I wasn't accepting any of the group help or psychologist recommendations offered by the firefighter community or anyone else trying to reach out to those who had worked at Ground Zero. Deep down, I knew that I really needed help. I knew that I couldn't just "John Wayne" it anymore. My life was unraveling day by day. I drank a little more than I normally did, which wasn't all that often at first. Then, over time, I began to empty more bottles. Every day I became more sluggish and useless.

I was very depressed. My sleep was interrupted by recurring nightmares that were very scary and intense, to say the least. I started taking naps during the day to compensate for the lack of sleep. I didn't exercise as much as I used to, and I started gaining weight. I stopped caring about my appearance and it was starting to show in various ways. I quickly became a cranky and difficult old man and I was still in my late forties.

Dr. Charles Carluccio was the key that helped me unlock and release my fears. We began to battle and defeat my ever-present nightmares. He helped me improve my relationships with my family and friends. He helped me start accepting strangers as I hadn't in years. Dr. Charles Carluccio saved my life.

After a few moments of silence, Dr. Carluccio finally spoke.

"I think I'm starting to notice a pattern here. Do you have a thing against cops?"

I looked up at him in disbelief. What did he mean by "pattern"? The whole reason I was talking with him in the first place was because a PATH sergeant, who was basically an officer, had sent me there. But as I eased back into my chair, I quickly remembered a previous story, a true story, that I had shared with him that might have made him draw that conclusion. In that story, everything was based on misunderstandings and assumptions. Things aren't always like that.

CHAPTER 10

FDNY REFLECTIONS

I was a *probie*, a first-year probationary firefighter fresh out of fire school, in my Midtown Manhattan firehouse, Ladder 4. We got a call to respond to a fire in an attached tenement, a five-story tenant walk-up only a few blocks from the firehouse. It was around 7:30 p.m., the time when almost everyone in New York is on 46th Street (the same street where the fire was) because the theaters were open. The famous New York performances were underway at the same time that the "Pride of Midtown" had to arrive at a performance of its own. No matter what it took, we weren't going to miss this fire. Our firehouse motto was "Never Miss a Performance."

Our chauffeur drove the truck the wrong way down 8th Avenue toward the 46th Street intersection so that we could be the first firehouse to reach the scene. We drove six blocks in the wrong direction and made a right turn that landed us in front of the building. I was sitting behind the chauffeur because I had the *can*. This meant that I would stay with the officer and carry the fire extinguisher when we went into the fire. When it was time for me to get out, I was on the side of the street facing the steps leading up to the front double doors of the building.

We rushed in and headed toward the open apartment door. Smoke poured out of it. Like so many Manhattan apartments, it was tiny, and from the doorway, we were already able to see the source of the smoke. It was a dinner gone wrong and everything on the stove top was smoking. It didn't help that the old building had raggedy cabinets that didn't do well when licked by flames from a kitchen fire.

Jack Guerci's job was to get to the roof and create a vent for the fire to move toward, thereby avoiding a situation in which the flames, because they had nowhere else to run from the water, reached out toward the firefighters actually holding the water hose. This meant that Jack had to trudge to the top of the huge building and make sure none of us below got into trouble.

He would probably take the adjoining building and either jump the roof or take the aerial ladder to the roof. However, running up the stairs is a lot faster than waiting for the aerial ladder to get set up. Now, I didn't see what was going on because I was on the right side and Jack was on the left side. He was supposed to be heading to the roof. The fire was almost out, but gray smoke was still in the hallway. Because the fire was in a tiny studio apartment, a person could take only two steps before hitting the back wall.

There really wasn't room to move in this place, so I stood in the hallway and straddled the threshold of the door while the other guys opened the window, pulled out the stove, and did whatever they had to do so they could maneuver. The officers talked to the guy who lived in the apartment and I was near the stairs. From there, I could look all the way down the forty-foot hallway and through the vestibule, or the small six-by-four-foot area with the mailboxes that sat between the outside door and the door to the building's interior. I saw Jack Guerci. I heard him arguing with two guys who looked like thugs. One guy was really tall, about six-foot-six—the kind of guy you have to climb a ladder to punch—and I could hear all of them screaming. I knew that something was about to happen.

I didn't know if I had the *can* in my hand, but I dropped the *can* and fell down on the wet, slippery floor. I quickly got back up and started running toward Jack because I knew everyone else was in the building; I was the only one who could see what was going on. I wasn't going to leave him out there alone. I blasted through the first door and heard the yelling getting louder. I saw Jack and the big guy squared off. The little guy positioned himself like he wanted to catch Jack off guard and hit him while Jack was focused on the big guy. I dove right through the door onto all of them.

I tackled the little guy because Jack had the big guy. We went right into the garbage pails. We grappled and wrestled and squared off. I grabbed the little guy and, as his coat opened up, I saw a gold badge hanging from his neck. I wasn't used to seeing cops wear their badges around their necks like that. While I was lying on the floor between Jack and the big guy, grabbing onto the little guy, I looked up the steps and yelled, "Jack! These guys are cops!"

It seemed like I'd said it in slow motion in a Sam Peckinpah Western because at that moment, Jack punched the big guy with a shot that sent blood all over the white tile. He almost knocked this guy out with one shot! I didn't know what was going on, but I knew that the big guy was still trying to hold Jack. The little guy had a gun and was trying to hold him too. My focus at the time was on holding down the little guy and keeping him and his gun off Jack.

Apparently, this all started when we had first arrived. Again, the chauffeur had gone the wrong way down the street so that we could get to the fire. Jack had gotten off the rig on the street side and I had gotten off on the sidewalk side. We knew that we had a fire and that we had to vent the roof, so the firehouse "Baby Huey," Jack, was the one who got that assignment. I had taken off running through the building with the officers who moved like jackrabbits to see who needed to be rescued inside and find the fire. Jack was left alone outside.

When Jack opened the door to get out, a black unmarked cop car squeezed him. He ripped the mirror off the car and threw it toward the car so he could get by and to the roof. The cops hit the brakes and got out of the car. The guy pulled a gun on Jack! Now, Jack didn't know who he was, but the detective was dressed in a black leather trench coat like members of the Irish Mafia wore at that time. The first thing Jack thought was not 'This guy is a cop' but 'This guy may be in the Mafia.' Jack slapped the hand of the guy holding the gun as if he were saying, "Get this thing out of the way! I have to get to the roof, and I don't have time for you or your gun!" Apparently, I showed up right after that.

Now the cop whom Jack had hit was crying, "I want that guy's job, I want him locked up!" Nine more cops were responding to a code 1013, which means "there's a cop in trouble." That's a code that sends other cops flying toward the scene. The fire department chiefs and additional fire trucks were coming in. I just knew we would have a huge mess on our hands.

As everyone started showing up, I was still lying on the floor; I wasn't letting go of this guy. Suddenly he started crying like a little girl and pointed at Jack. "He hit me!" I couldn't believe that this guy who had been trying to tear off my head a few minutes earlier was now crying like a victim. Both officers were taken to Bellevue Hospital. One of them may have had a broken nose. No charges were pressed against me, but Jack ended up in lock-up.

We finished the job and had a few more calls that night, so it was 6 a.m. before we showed up at the precinct with the rig to pick him up. We had to work our way through the news teams in front of the firehouse. They wanted exclusive interviews so they could have more information than what had already appeared in the newspaper that day.

When I walked in, I saw Jack smoking his favorite Chesterfield cigarettes while three other guys huddled together in the corner of the cell. I don't know what happened over the course of the evening, but it was clear they didn't want anything to do with Jack. He had been in a cell before, I'm sure. And the fact that the cops hadn't taken the handcuffs off him spoke volumes!

The chief started talking to him like Jack was a five-year-old, explaining what he shouldn't be doing! By now news teams were taking pictures of him in handcuffs—photos that would accompany stories about a Brooklyn firefighter who had gotten into a fight with a cop!

Jack was on a modified assignment until everything blew over. I remember there was talk about a court date, but nothing came of it as far as I know.

I assumed that this story made Dr. Carluccio think that I had a thing against cops, but that wasn't the case. I'll admit that I was amazed by how Jack had fought that day. He had delivered a punch that had made me feel like I was standing next to Muhammad Ali or Joe Frazier! What a shot! One shot, just one! But as the son of a retired NYPD officer and the friend of many other officers, I can't say that I have anything against all cops—just those particular cops who had gone after my firehouse brother, Jack.

Maybe I should have told Dr. Carluccio about the time I went to lunch with Petey, a highway patrol officer. Judy and I both consider Peter Ferrara to be our best friend. He was even the best man at our wedding. Pete grew up around the corner from me on 69th Street and 19th Avenue. I've known him since I was twelve years old. We've been so close for so long that he has been referred to as my mom's sixth son.

It was either Da Vinci's on 18th Avenue or L & B Spumoni

Gardens—those were the final lunch choices for the day as Petey quickly wielded his sporty 380 Z when we left my house on Bay 37th Street in Bensonhurst, Brooklyn. As we passed Mama Mia's pizza on Bath Avenue, only two blocks from our destination, I was tempted to tell Pete to pull over the Z-car for a quick slice that would put a dent in my tremendous hunger pangs. I'd gotten up early and sustained myself throughout the day with coffee, so now that it was about 3 p.m., I was starving! I decided against it, knowing that Pete's expert driving skills would have us safely in front of Da Vinci's in a few minutes. Still, I couldn't resist urging him to maximize his NYPD highway cop experience and put the pedal to the metal. If his rocket ship had had lights and sirens, I would have turned them on myself.

While riding past Mama Mia's, I eagerly looked inside to see if Mario was pulling a fresh pie from the oven. If he was, I definitely had to ask Petey to stop. But as I straightened my head to look forward again, something strange caught my eye in the nanosecond it took to cross Bay 35th Street. I thought I saw an all-too-familiar sight of heavy black smoke far down the block. With an urgency similar to what I would have shown had we just run over Miss America, I hollered at Pete to stop. The Z-car abruptly did.

"I thought you were starving. What's up?"

"Quick backup! We have to take a look down Bay 35th Street," was the only explanation I offered.

He quickly responded and a few seconds later was speeding down Bay 35th Street, a one-way, in the wrong direction. People in the street and on the sidewalk were screaming as flames and black smoke protruded from the open front door and top floor of the two-story attached brick building. Pete quickly pulled the Z-car across the street from the burning building in an unofficial parking spot that blocked someone's driveway.

We rushed across the street, up the steps, and through the open door while women and children outside screamed that children were trapped upstairs in the burning apartment. I didn't have time for even a quick size-up through the black smoke that immediately met us in the vestibule; instead, I relied on what I knew about the buildings in that area. I knew the steps would be to the left even though I couldn't see them. As we bolted up the stairs, we heard the screaming and crying of kids at the top of the stairs.

Thank God one of the kids, a petrified and crying little girl about four years old, was at the top of the steps waiting for us. I quickly grabbed her and handed her to Pete before I crawled on my belly past a burning room just a few feet from the top of the stairs. I saw another child in the hallway, lying on the floor in front of me. The girl looked like she was about six years old and she was coughing and crying. When I finally reached her, I scooped her up, crawled back to Pete, and handed off the second child. I told him to get downstairs and out of the burning building.

In the distance, I heard sirens and knew that help was on its way. I crawled into a rear bedroom whose door was open. The orange flames lit up the room, giving me a good view. I was blessed that the fire was already venting through the open windows at the rear of the room. I was able to search and look in and under the bed, then take a quick look in the closet before my seared lungs burned with such intensity that I knew I was totally spent. I crawled headfirst to the top of the stairs and slid down as Pete reentered the building.

"Get the hell out of there!" he yelled as he clambered up the stairs and pulled my outstretched arm, dramatically increasing the speed of my sliding retreat. The people on the street had informed him that no one was left inside except me. Pete had placed the two children safely in the custody of a neighbor directly across the street from the flame-enveloped building. We knew that if we didn't get the car out of the driveway, we would be trapped by the incoming rigs responding to the fire from both directions on the one-way street. So, we dashed back to the Z-car and Peter pulled out of the block just as one of the first to arrive was headed our way. We narrowly passed the first due engine that was racing to the fire.

When the fire-charged adrenaline gradually subsided, my attention returned to the void in my stomach. I inhaled that first square of delicious Da Vinci's pizza so quickly, it barely touched my lips. I started working on the second square probably about the same time that the first due Engine 253 "Bensonhurst's Bravest" company that we passed had extinguished the fire. I smiled to myself as I reflected on the moments leading up to our casual lunch. Great job, Brother Pete!

I had written my "Teddy the Firebug" story only because it was something Dr. Carluccio himself had recommended as part of my therapy. He challenged me to write stories as a way for me to get used to expressing myself again. I had pretty much shut down after my FDNY brotherhood ostracized me. What else was I supposed to do when almost half the people I had known throughout my adult life had been killed in the collapse of the Twin Towers and the other half didn't want to bother with me because they saw me as a robber of widows and orphans? After all that, I can't say I was exactly an open and trusting guy.

"Well, I'm glad to know that you don't have anything against cops," Dr. Carluccio said, interrupting my thoughts. "But are any of the events in your story true?"

Now, that was a good question. A lot of crazy things have happened in my firehouses over the years. And like most writers, I had gleaned parts of the story from actual events. For example, Bobby Fash had a few things in common with Teddy.

When I became a firefighter, I had just moved. I lived in a brand-new, three-story building under the Verrazano Bridge, right on the water on Shore Road. My girlfriend and I lived on the top floor. When you're a firefighter candidate, like in the police department, you wear a different kind of uniform and you have a bag; they know you're going to school. The cop uniforms are usually gray, and it's the same in the fire department. One day, as I was running into the building, a guy on his way out turned to look at me. He said, "Hey, how you doing?"

"Hey, how you doing?" I replied. "You live here?"

"Yeah, I'm living here."

"Oh, that's cool. You work out in Manhattan?"

"Yeah, I work in Manhattan."

"What's your name?"

"Bobby Fash."

"Oh, cool. Where are you?"

"I'm in *Probie School*."

"Okay, cool."

And that was the end of the conversation. He was moving out, so I saw him only once or twice. I didn't know whether he was getting divorced at the time. I really didn't know what his story was. He had the studio apartment on the first floor while I had the big apartment on the third floor. All I knew was that I had met him while I was in *Probie School* and that when I got out and walked in the door of 4 Truck, where I was assigned, I saw the same guy I had met in my building: Bobby Fash. He was in the firehouse! He was assigned to Ladder 4 with me!

And he was a Rockaway guy. He was a great swimmer. Bobby had grown up on the beach in Rockaway and could swim in the ocean for miles. He was a really nice, quiet guy with a barrel chest, and he was as strong as an ox. I wondered how quickly he could knock down doors. The guy was tough!

He wasn't a good drinker, though. One day, when he wasn't working, he went to a nice Irish bar right across the street from the firehouse. We used to cash our paychecks there. It was more like a dive with the classic dirty windows, smoky atmosphere, and old furniture but as long as it served alcohol, no one cared about all that. All the off-duty firefighters went there to cash their checks, drink, and hang out. That was exactly what Bobby was doing at the bar.

I was scheduled to come in the next morning, so I wasn't at the house or on the payday bar crawl. When I parked across the street for my morning shift, I noticed that the big, old, wooden doors on this bar looked like they had been hacked and that the bar was entirely boarded up. I immediately assumed that there had been a fire. I didn't smell the remnants of a fire, but what else could it have been?

As I walked through the firehouse, I noticed that everybody had a deadpan expression. That was when I knew something terrible had happened. Over and over, I asked, "What is going on?" All I heard in response was "Umhmm. Umhmm. Don't want to be the first one to tell you." By this point, I absolutely had to know what was going on. Because no one was telling me anything, I started making the coffee. When the rest of the guys started talking, I outright demanded to know what was going on.

"You know Bobby Fash?" asked one of the senior firefighters.

"Yeah, Bobby Fash what?" Now I was worried that he may have been injured on a call.

"Bobby Fash was in the bar last night," he sighed in a matter-of-fact voice. "With everybody else. I don't know if he stayed with his friends, or a couple of friends, and maybe one was a cop, which was fine, I don't know. At some point, they turned to Bobby Fash and said, 'You're cut off. You're done.'"

If one of the guys was drinking and lived far away, he could always sleep in the firehouse. No one cared if he was there and it wasn't his tour so long as he wasn't interfering with the guys who were on at that time. We always did it. You'd go to a ball game, or a party, or a hockey game and you'd get out late, and you'd go to the firehouse so you wouldn't have to drive. It wasn't a written rule or department policy, but we were all aware of that perk. Naturally, that was where I assumed Bobby Fash ended up, but that wasn't exactly the case.

So, they'd tried to throw him out.

"You ain't throwing me out! My money's good!" Bobby had yelled at the bartender.

Mike had said, "Go ahead, you got to get out. No more drinking. You told me only one more!"

"Oh, no!" Bobby had shouted back.

And then they had tried throwing him out. A big guy had tried to force Bobby out of the bar, but Bobby had started fighting with him. Finally, they had thrown Bobby out the door, then locked the door behind them. By now it was 4 a.m., which was the normal closing time for bars in Manhattan.

"I ain't done drinkin'!" Bobby had shouted.

Eventually, Bobby walked toward the firehouse. The firefighters with him had taken off and gone home. They'd all assumed that everything was settled for the night. But what did Bobby do? He'd gone into the firehouse, taken the axe out of the rig, gone back across the street, and tried to chop down the bar's door! Before he managed to get completely through the door, the cops had arrived and locked him up.

He was a quiet guy! He never had words with any guy. He was kind of soft-spoken, not opinionated. He wasn't one of the guys you would expect to pull a stunt like that. I didn't know that he was a nasty drunk.

The bar didn't press charges but they did make Bobby pay for the doors. Obviously, he wasn't allowed to come back into the bar. And everybody pretended it hadn't happened. At least we did until the firehouse phone started ringing with calls from the other firehouses. "Hey, man, is Bobby Fash around?"

"Yeah, he's right here," the house watchman covering the phone would answer.

"No, he's across the street having a drink. We want our axe back!"

They were clowns. A firehouse down the street even blocked their number and called us to say, "When he gets out of jail, tell him to bring the axe back!" And that was the way it went. He still worked with us even though he got locked up for ten minutes.

I guess you could say that I got some of my story about Teddy from actual events, even though they didn't necessarily involve me. Dr. Carluccio asked me a few other questions about the Teddy story and then we moved onto other topics.

"Did most of the firefighters you were closest to spend time in lock-up?" Dr. Carluccio asked without looking up from his clipboard.

Oh no. I could see where this was going. The colorful stories involving lock-up are usually the easiest to remember; that's why I ended up sharing them with Dr. Carluccio first. It wasn't like everyone I associated with ended up in lock-up. Even those who did were still good people; they just made poor decisions and were caught. I could tell that I had to set Dr. Carluccio straight on that, and soon. So, I told him about a few of the guys I'd met throughout the years the years— guys guys whom I looked up to.

Bobby Gunn sang "Danny Boy" the best I'd ever heard it. He used to make the bar cry when he sang a cappella. He held your attention whether you liked the song or not. He used to go to the bar across the street and, after throwing down more than a few cold ones and reaching the point where his nose was nice and red like Rudolph the Red-Nosed Reindeer's, this fifty-year-old engine guy would start singing while the bar was packed! It wasn't one of those dainty martini joints. And all these old Irish guys…oh, he'd take the bartenders from the other side, that was the joint. You know, the Westies were tough, all of the West Side was like that…and the bar went silent after two notes!

Silence! I mean, silence! I mean, about one hundred guys were there and not one of them made a sound! These guys stood like they were at attention! They were just listening. Bobby could sing this song in the best voice you ever heard. I had never even heard of the song and I was starting to wonder what it was, but I didn't say anything because I knew someone would have been ready to slap me! Bobby was singing this song, and the guys were crying!

He didn't do it all the time, he really didn't. People would ask him to perform it, but he would never sing it. It had to be the right moment. I caught it a few times, and he would sing it at functions and whatnot. Since I first heard Bobby sing it, I have heard other guys sing it a million times, but Bobby's version is still the best I've ever heard. Man, he could sing!

Bobby worked part-time as a bank teller. When he retired from the FDNY, he was promoted to bank manager, but he had serious talent as a singer.

Mike Wernick was another guy with talent. He was the guy who attended Columbia Architect School's graduate program to become an architect while working in the world's biggest firehouse. He was a Jewish guy and he'd been a wrestler in college. He was a little guy, a tough guy, and an all-around great guy. He used to stay up all night with pots of coffee in the basement while he built little models and then took his tests. He eventually became a full-fledged architect while he was a firefighter.

Mike married an Asian woman, Nuri, from the Philippines. No kids. He was one of my best friends. He was my conscience. "You can't do that," he used to tell me. He was a calm, quiet guy. Smart. And he lived in the village around the corner from the Hell's Angels on the Lower East Side before it was trendy. Then he moved around the corner. As his second job, he managed New York City's only indoor motorcycle parking garage. Another guy owned it, but Mike ran it. And he lived above it. It was a loft and it was very beautiful. In the back was an open deck with French doors. He really made this place wonderful. It was quiet; you'd never hear the motorcycles rustling or making noise. He used to take me there to show me some of the most beautiful motorcycles. A lot of heavy-hitter musicians' bikes were there. I don't know whether Bob Dylan's motorcycle was there, but big, heavy-duty people brought their bikes in, whether they used them or not.

You weren't allowed to wash your bike and you weren't allowed to start your bike inside. You had to wheel it outside. He had all these rules. The place was called "Rising Wolf Motors." Everybody had their helmets and jackets and stuff. You couldn't work on the bikes in there, either. No oil changes or any of that. But everybody had a locker, like in the firehouse. All open. Nothing was closed and nobody stole anything. There had to have been 100 to 150 motorcycles in there. This was on both sides of the building, front to rear. It was a big place. As of the time of this writing, the place still exists! In fact, Mike ended up buying the business and the building! He's an architect and a firefighter who happens to run a motorcycle shop. The guy is unbelievable!

I think he wants to build a building above the building to give himself more space. It's a good thing that he knows an architect who can design something like that.

Mike was also a 9/11 survivor. When I transferred to Brooklyn, he transferred to the 9 Truck on Great Jones Street so he could walk to work. He told me that the trip took about 143 steps. They had the biggest firehouse in the city, or at least one of them. They also had the longest pole in the city, one from the third floor to the first floor. You had to be careful with that one. Oops! That was a huge firehouse! And in the basement were giant stalls that served as lockers. I mean, giant stalls that were more like rooms. Mike kept his architecture books and papers in there. He also had a desk, lamps chairs, and a couch. It was amazing!

In a sense, he did his work at the firehouse. But he was a brilliant guy, a great guy. He drove the truck for Ladder 9. The truck was severely damaged, but it wasn't one of the trucks that had been crushed. A couple of guys in the company whom he worked with died, but he survived.

I remember going to a couple of tough fires with Mike. He was a very good firefighter. He made his bones in Brooklyn's Engine 207, then turned to the dark side and went to Midtown's 4 Truck. He was always "all in" with the big guys who would pull the ceilings, force the doors and do everything else that had to happen. He was strong and always in great shape.

He also responded to the Trade Center bombing in 1993. His ladder was probably second or third *due* down there. The necessity of operating in unsettled, chaotic conditions was so common, these professionals masterfully took it in stride.

I took my kids to Mike and Nori's. The motorcycle collection shocked them. "He's so cool," they said as they went up to Mike's apartment.

Nori is a professional masseuse who specializes in prenatal massages. She had set up the room like an old Chinese pagoda. From the kitchen, one could see a big wooden deck that went over the back of the garage. It was really cool. Mike and Nori took motorcycle trips all over the world. They've been to every continent!

Plenty of firefighters trained for and worked second jobs as plumbers, technicians, contractors, and even lawyers, but Mike was the first and only firefighting architect I ever met.

Once I had convinced Dr. Carluccio that everyone with whom I socialized during my firefighter days wasn't a convict, he wrapped up our session and I headed home.

Dr. Carluccio was the first psychiatrist I visited but he wasn't the last. Since 2002, I have shared my story with therapists who have helped me get past the debilitating and severe depression and extreme pangs of loneliness so that I can pick up the pieces and keep going. It has been a process of reinvention. And although I wasn't Teddy the Firebug, considering the path I was on before I started seeing the psychiatrist, I could have ended up like Teddy.

Dr. Carluccio was the determining factor in helping me move forward and face my challenge of riding in traffic tunnels and bridges. Without facing this fear, I never would have been able to become one of the volunteers at the Tribute Center. They started talking about it in 2003. Because the official memorial wouldn't be completed until 2009, the Tribute Center was being promoted as an "interim destination" where members of the 9/11 community, which included the survivors, residents, rescue and recovery workers, volunteers, and family members, could tell their personal stories to visitors and provide details about the fight to reach the 2,973 lives that were lost on that day. The advertised mission was to inspire healing, and that was something I needed. I had to be a part of Tribute, and Dr. Carluccio helped make that possible for me.

I hadn't returned to that site since January 6, 2002, when I left kicking and screaming, wanting to stay until I felt my job was done, but it wasn't my decision to make. However, it was my decision to return and share the stories of my friends and what had happened to them on that fateful day. It was my decision to speak to the thousands of visitors who were projected to go through the Tribute each day and to explain what I had seen, what my role was, and what I had experienced. Most of all, it was my decision to be there to thank the visitors for their blessings and their support for all of us who had taken part in America's history. Unbeknownst to them, their love and support had gotten me through the toughest times while I worked at Ground Zero. I had to personally thank them. I needed this to help heal myself, too.

CHAPTER 11

RISING FROM ASHES

At first it was very difficult for me to become a docent for the Tribute Center at Ground Zero. It took a lot just to muster up the courage to return to the scene of the crime, not to mention the drive to get there from New Jersey. It was very emotional for me to personally thank all the people for their support. One person I was especially interested in thanking was a fearless woman named Kimberly Krieger, whom I had first met in the days immediately following the collapse of the towers.

She had left her full-time job so that she could spend her days and evenings there at Ground Zero serving the rescue workers as a Red Cross volunteer. I saw her each time I went to one of the recovery stations to get oxygen or water. She was always there to give us food, water, a blanket, someone to talk to, or whatever we could possibly need. I had participated in the Ground Zero rescue and recovery from September 11, 2001 to January 6, 2002, and I saw her there every single day. So, I shouldn't have been surprised to have seen her working again with the Tribute Center.

To reconnect with the people who had helped me during the times when I needed it most was one experience, but to make the trip to see nothing but a giant hole in the ground was quite another. It was truly amazing. I couldn't do it as much as I wanted to because of the emotional toll it took on me. Yet with the constant and persistent counsel and encouragement of Dr. Carluccio, it became a good part of my therapy.

Just before the Tribute Center opened, I agreed to take small steps that would help me get out of the house before I took the big step of volunteering at the Tribute. I joined something called the Optimist Club. It was my local chapter of a worldwide organization dedicated to serving the communities in which we lived. We would raise money to send children with cancer to a one-week summer camp where they could get out of the hospital rooms where so many of them had spent most of their days. They could enjoy spending time doing activities that would make them smile and that would allow them to interact with other children while they still had access to a 24/7 team of nine on-duty volunteer nurses and an oncologist.

Not only did I help raise money to send fifty youth up to age seventeen to the camp, but I also spent the last week of June 2006 serving on the security team. The kids were always in groups of at least two and a counselor was always with each of them. During the camp, they had the opportunity to experience everything that their diagnosis permitted, from riding in hot air balloons to zip lining to participating in a game show to watching performances of professional jugglers and demonstrations by animal handlers. It was amazing and I was so happy to be a part of it that I continued working with the program for a few more years.

For almost three decades I had always adopted children in need through World Vision, but there was something special about being physically present at those summer camps with the children. The experience made me think about saving money so that I could travel to Africa and visit with one of my adopted children. However, after I calculated the cost of travel, I thought it best to use the money to adopt another child and make a difference in another life rather than spend thousands to travel to a country and spend a few hours with a child who would probably be nervous and apprehensive about communicating with me. I ended up doing just that, adopting a child in South America and being content with sending letters and reading the ones they wrote to me.

These experiences taught me how powerful giving is in the healing process. Yet it was an adventure in Philadelphia that showed me another side of giving.

My wife and kids were out of town and my mind buzzed with the possibilities of what to do. This was a freedom I hadn't experienced in a while. I took the last two nickels that I had saved for a rainy day and decided that it was finally pouring and time to shoot the wad! My lifelong favorite team, the New York Rangers, is an arch-rival of Philadelphia and was about to play them for the top spot in the division. The Flyers were undefeated at home that season and I knew this was going to be a sold-out game.

After a two-hour drive to Philadelphia, I arrived with the hope of buying a single ticket. I knew to keep my lucky Rangers jersey under wraps just long enough to procure a ticket. There was no sense in letting the ticket scalper know that I wasn't a local. The price would increase astronomically if they suspected that I had come from New York to attend the game. I was blessed to find a legal parking spot on the street very close to the arena and saved twenty dollars on a paid parking lot. This left me with more funds for ticket negotiations. They were beginning to love me in Philadelphia.

As I walked through the parking lot, I spotted a bona fide ticket agent hiding in the shadows.

"Tickets," he whispered.

"What you got? I only need one," I said.

"Section 107 behind the goal. Row 13. Gimme a buck and a quarter."

"Forty bucks," I quickly responded as I started to walk past him. I knew that I would have to be sharp.

"Seventy-five," he shot back.

"Only got a fifty. Who wants it? I don't care where the seats are, I just want to get in," I said. I also reminded him that there were only twelve minutes left until face-off.

"Done deal," he quickly concluded to avoid losing a sale to another scalper.

I made a silent exchange after examining the validity of the tickets: Section 107. Row 13. Seat 3. Directly behind the Ranger goal with an eighty-nine dollar face value. I chose that time to reveal my lucky Rangers jersey commemorating the 1993-1994 Stanley Cup Championship win. The first time I boldly wore it had been to the game seven finals on the enchanted evening in June 1994 when I witnessed the fifty-four-year drought come to an end as the New York Rangers finally won the Stanley Cup. This was the same lucky Rangers jersey that I wore to the game in Philadelphia.

"Thanks, brother!" I said to the bewildered scalper who had just learned that I had gotten the better of him.

And with that, the true blessing began. I could now profess the meaning of the City of Brotherly Love!

You haven't completely experienced life as a sports fan if you haven't been to a major rival game in the insanely crazy sports town of Philadelphia while proudly wearing your team colors, the enemy's colors. The vile profanity, rage, anger, threats, and gestures only multiplied as I chanted, "Let's Go Rangers," over and over while deep in the Flyers' lair.

As I descended to find my seat, the furious Flyers fans screamed at the top of their lungs in an effort to drown me out. This effort was aided by an aerial assault of peanuts and partially full beer cups that mysteriously managed to hit only me and not the people around me. Not at all bothered, I turned and welcomed the onslaught.

The first period ended in a typical hard-fought and knuckle-crushing one-all tie. Between the periods, I was able to catch a fan-favorite t-shirt fired off the ice by a beautiful Flyer cheerleader. By this time, I knew that they loved me in Philadelphia. I shared my new rolled-up t-shirt love story with all who were within earshot.

The second period ended in a two-all tie. During the second stanza intermission, there was an announcement over the public address system that all fans sitting in Section 107 had won a remote-controlled car courtesy of the Flyers.

"Go to Gate 120 and show your ticket stub to collect your prize."

I did just that. Now that I had scored free parking, a thirty-five dollar savings on a ticket right behind my team's goal, a t-shirt, and a remote-controlled car, I knew that they loved me in Philadelphia!

The official Flyers photographer followed me and photographed me as I accepted my new toy. I detected a particular disdain as he carried out his obligatory duties, but I was more concerned with a greater potential problem. My raging and close-quartered neighbors now had two periods of drinking under their belts, and I anticipated additional attacks with their freshened artillery. The toy car came with a small box of batteries. I didn't mind being pelted with peanuts but flying batteries would surely do damage.

Once I made it back to my seat, I spotted a young boy who was wearing his Flyers jersey and sitting beside his dad in Section 106, in the first and second seats off the aisle. They had missed winning the car by one section.

I introduced myself as a retired firefighter from New York City and handed the boy a small photo taken of me at Ground Zero on September 11th. I told him to be a true fan and to always be loyal to his team, the Philadelphia Flyers. He looked like he was about nine or ten years old. I told him that I had become a Rangers fan when I was around that age. I continued to tell him how I had endured the pain of the losses and the thrills of the wins for forty years and how he too would experience that with his team. Then I gave him the remote-controlled car and the t-shirt.

I turned to return to my seat and the Flyers fans who had witnessed the brief encounter erupted into cheers that were just as energetic as when the Flyers scored a goal. They accepted me as a good guy who was just wearing the wrong jersey.

On my long drive back home, I reflected on how great America is… and how great it is to have your team win 4-3 in an overtime shootout in the opponent's hometown. That day, I learned that Philadelphia really is the City of Brotherly Love and that there really is something powerful about giving to others.

The co-founders of the Tribute Center understood the power of giving back, and I was glad to be able, and mentally prepared, to do so. The $3.4 million facility was housed in a Liberty Street storefront that had once been a deli directly across the street from the World Trade Center. It had also been next door to an FDNY firehouse. It featured four galleries that introduced visitors to life on Radio Row before September 11th, offered information about the February 26, 1993 bombing of the World Trade Center, connected them with the people and events of September 11, 2001, and gave them a chance to reflect on their own experiences. It was a touching tribute designed and managed by the men and women whose lives were personally touched by that fateful day—and I was one of the men who was able to volunteer there.

On September 6, 2006, three years after the co-founders had developed the idea for the center, a private opening was held for the 9/11 community of survivors and family members of those who were murdered on that day. It was a solemn, tearful, yet somehow tranquil day as we gathered to remember the lives we lost and embrace our lives as those who survived. We were all in various stages of healing but being together made an impact that I hadn't anticipated. On September 20, the Tribute Center would be open to the public, but this day was for us.

During one of the tours I gave on that special day for the 9/11 community, I learned about a man in a red bandana whom I will never forget. Each of the docents was assigned a different spot in the Center so that we could explain each section. Near where I stood was a photo of Welles Crowther. When his mother, father, and sister came through, his mother explained more of his story to me.

Welles had been a volunteer firefighter in his pre-college days in Nyack, New York, a stone's throw from Manhattan. After having earned a degree from Boston College, he had been in the South Tower as an equity trader. When news arrived of the first plane landing in the North Tower, a college roommate had called Welles to check on him and had learned that he was heading out of the South Tower following a building-wide announcement. That was the last contact he had with family and friends, but Welles spent the last hour of his life helping others escape the South Tower after it, too, was hit. The people he helped didn't know his name. They only knew that he wore a red bandana. When Welles' mother heard the reports of a man with a red bandana who had helped people escape, she knew that it was her son, who had worn the red bandana since his father had given it to him when Welles was six years old.

Following September 11th, Welles' father went to Welles' Manhattan apartment to collect his personal belongings. While in the apartment, his father found a printed-out and unsigned application for the New York City Fire Department. It was still awaiting the inclusion of a college transcript. Welles was going to give up his career as an affluent equities trader to become a firefighting city employee.

Welles was a man who had gone to work as a pawn. He was there to do the work his supervisors had assigned to him. However, he ended the day, and his life, as a warrior. In a matter of moments, he made up his mind to change his fate. He may have survived had he simply left the tower, but he chose to take the cards he was dealt and do something different with them.

In his memory, his family started something called the Welles Remy Crowther Charitable Trust, which benefits young people. Each year they host an annual golf classic. There are races, concerts, and a list of other events that bring awareness to different issues affecting youth. They also tell more people about their son and continue to make an impact like Welles did on September 11th.

Before the Crowther family left the Tribute Center on that special day for 9/11 family members, we exchanged contact information and offered to help each other in any way possible. I knew that they had put a lot of work into their causes and had raised a lot of money for kids, so they already had my attention. But when they called and invited me to play, of all things, ice hockey for their cause, there was no way I could turn that down.

Welles had been a hockey player in high school and a lacrosse player at Boston College, so his high school team had come up with the idea of hosting a reunion game and inviting Welles' college lacrosse team members to play as well. The Crowther family remembered me and my love of hockey, and they let me have the honor of being the slowest and fattest player on the ice. I loved it!

We were broken down into two teams: the White Team and the Black Team. I was on the White Team and I even had my own jersey. I didn't keep the jersey, though. I gave it back to them so they could auction it off. I wanted them to have anything they could make money off of. It wasn't mine, anyway (though I did manage to get a picture of me out on the ice, waiting for the game to start). Both teams wore identical jerseys in different colors that said, "Welles Crowther" on them.

Everybody got on the ice wearing a red bandana at the beginning and we played a good game. The Black Team really gave it to my team, but it was all for a good cause. The event was covered in the news and in the newspapers. I couldn't believe how much money they had been able to raise just so they could give it away. They even sold jerseys and hats that professional athletes had signed. They were definitely noticed in their area and they did a lot in memory of their son—the guy who could have been a multi-millionaire but who wanted to be a firefighter instead.

I volunteered as a docent at the Tribute Center for a couple of years after I met the Crowther family. I met a lot of families who chose to do things in honor of their fallen loved ones, but none were quite like this family. You might even say that meeting them inspired me to do more in honor of my fallen firefighters and to represent them on any occasion I could.

I was honored to be invited by the United States Navy to take part in the christening of United States ship LPD 21, *U.S.S. New York*: the newest concept in the modern Navy. This ship class was specifically designed to combat the kind of modern terrorism that ended the lives of 2,973 people on September 11, 2001. The christening was to be held in New Orleans, Louisiana. Getting to New Orleans had been on my short list for some thirty years, but the christening finally pulled it all together for me. I had missed the road trip there with my uncle, his children, and my older brother Charlie back in the summer of 1968, but this time I had to make it.

During the forty-five-minute bus ride from New Orleans to the shipbuilding yard in Avondale, Louisiana, I thought about my dad, who had served aboard a liberty ship, a branch of the United States Navy, during World War II as a US Merchant Marine. I caught a brief glimpse of the ship as the bus rolled down the tree-lined hill past its checkpoints. The *U.S.S. New York* proudly wore the number "21" on her hull. That was the same year my father was born.

Tears ran down my face as I gazed at the ship in all her honor and glory. Seven tons of steel debris from the World Trade Center had been brought here, melted down, and embedded into the spine of the ship's mighty core. The *U.S.S. New York* was specifically designed to transport and deploy 800 US Marines under the cloak of invisible stealth. Her latest state-of-the-art training drills during transport prepared these brave warriors, ensuring they would be ready for deployment at a moment's notice and armed to the teeth with all the necessary equipment stowed within the ship's confines.

As the magnum-sized champagne bottle cracked across her majestic bow, the flags, banners, and streaming ribbons came alive, dancing to the Pipes and Drums of the FDNY and the sounds of the NYPD band. More tears flooded my eyes because I knew that the ship would serve stealthily and swiftly. The insurgents who hid behind rocks and deeply dug caves in faraway places would be overtaken. Not all too soon, they would utterly regret that they had taken sides against the United States of America.

CHAPTER 12

CHIEFS, PAWNS & WARRIORS

Before September 11, 2001, one of the greatest things I had ever done was sneak into Madison Square Garden to watch my beloved New York Rangers play for the 1993-1994 Stanley Cup. The Rangers hadn't won the Stanley Cup in fifty-four years, since 1940. I desperately wanted to go to the game. I had no money, no tickets, nothing that could have gotten me anywhere near that game. Those tickets sold for a minimum of $2,500 to over $5,000 for one seat anywhere in the building. I tried like heck. I knew I was off that night. I was nervous for my team. I scrambled and I didn't know what to do.

Then it dawned on me that I had done hundreds of building inspections in Manhattan. I thought that I could possibly pull this off if I put on my Class A uniform. I borrowed a clipboard from the firehouse and put some old building inspection paperwork, cards, and guidelines from the office on it. It was all official paperwork, but it wasn't filled out for Madison Square Garden and it wouldn't be submitted like a real inspection. Now I was ready to go.

I had to get there really early because I knew that when they did these inspections, if the game started at 7:30 or 7:00, you'd have to be in that building by about 4:30. I went in through the side entrance. You don't go through the gate to the front door, you go underneath the Garden where the players enter. There was all kinds of security down there and that's where the owners come in. It's a really big deal to get through. However, I was wearing my Class A uniform and my hat, carrying my official clipboard with the peach-colored building card. Because this was a public venue, the Garden staff knew that they were going to be inspected. This was a common occurrence for them, so the people in security expected the fire department to show up, as well as special details from the police department and whoever else.

When I entered, I saw no fewer than two captains, three chiefs, and a chief's aide going into the Garden. They were probably doing the same thing I was, except they got a free meal. I piggy-backed off of them. They didn't really see me because I came up from behind them; I waited a bit to see when I could make my move. When they went through security, they were met by a detail of Madison Square Garden officials, who guided them to where they had to go.

They entered a bank of elevators and I shortened the gap between us to make sure I could still get in. All of a sudden, a guy from the detail hosting the captains, the chiefs, and the chief's aide turned around and looked at me.

"Is this guy with you?"

They all turned and saw me in my Class A's, then looked at me with puzzled expressions on their faces. But somehow the chief's aide remembered me. I only vaguely remembered him. He was an older guy who must have had at least twenty-five years on the job. I think he was a chief's aide in the 7th Battalion. I was in the 9th Battalion, so our firehouses couldn't have been too far from each other. The chief's aide actually called my name.

"Hey, Ron! Yeah, he's with us."

Just like that. And then he gave me one of those eyebrow movements telling me that he was going to cover me to get me in but that I wasn't welcome to go with them because he had already done what he could for me.

I took the hint and didn't get into the elevator with him; I took another one instead. I had to pretend that I was walking around the Garden, checking exits. I didn't really care what I had to do because I was in the building now. I was in and had free reign. I didn't have a ticket or a seat, but it didn't matter.

Where did I go? It was about 4:45 p.m. and the game wasn't scheduled to start for at least two hours. The fans hadn't even been let in yet. I decided to go up to the lounge. I had never been invited up there because that's where the zillion-dollar seats are located. I found it after asking some of the workers. I took another elevator to go up a few more flights and reach the lounge area. Remember, once you get past security and into the building, you have free reign because no one else is going to ask you what you're doing—especially if you're in uniform.

When I arrived, I found a very large and very nice bar area and restaurant. I didn't have any money for that, so I wasn't interested in staying. But while I was up there, I ran into Mike Francesa, one of the most famous sports radio announcers. At the time, he was co-host of the popular "Mike and the Mad Dog" radio show. Now he has his own radio program. He was in the radio business for maybe thirty years, and he was one of those people who was always at major games like this.

"Hey, Mike! How are you doing?"

"Alright," he replied when he saw me.

All this time I had been carrying a shopping bag. I sat down with

Mike and chatted with him for a moment.

"The Rangers are going to win the Cup tonight," I proudly announced.

Mike just looked at me.

"I guarantee the Rangers are going to win the Cup. Look at what I've got."

I opened the shopping bag and showed him my brand-new white New York Rangers jersey with these words on the back: "Stanley Cup 1993-1994 Champs." It's falling apart now but I still have it, and it's what I showed Mike that day. I've worn it occasionally since then. In fact, it was the same jersey I wore when I attended the Rangers game in Philadelphia, where I'd given the t-shirt and remote-controlled car to the young boy.

I knew the shirt would be garbage if the Rangers lost that night, but I had confidence. I also had a key ingredient in my bag next to the jersey. I had my ice skates with the special blade covers made out of old rubber firefighter boots. They were a key part of my plan. When the Rangers won the Stanley Cup, I was going to put on my jersey and skates and then wait until the Cup came out to go out on the ice with my team. I was going to grab the Cup as a fan favorite of New York City. I didn't care what was going on because that's what I was going to do. That was the major plan. Yet in the meantime, I knew that I needed a place to hide. So, I said my goodbyes to Mike. I never spoke to him again, but I'll never forget having met him that day.

I went around the Garden with my shopping bag, then decided to look for a seat all the way upstairs, where the skyboxes were located. I knew these seats were impregnable and that a person couldn't just walk in there. Security was everywhere and I didn't know any of those people. I walked into one room and saw a lady sitting in the front row. I didn't recognize her, but I quickly learned that she was Emily Griffiths, wife of the late Frank Griffiths (who had founded the Vancouver Canucks) and mother of Arthur Griffiths, the Vancouver Canucks president. She saw me come in with my Class A's and she must have assumed that I had an official reason for being there.

"How are you? Come on in!" she invited me. Then she motioned for me to have a seat. I introduced myself and tried to get comfortable. It was unbelievable to get seats like this, but I was a Rangers fan and couldn't watch the Stanley Cup game in enemy territory. Fortunately, someone came in to give me the perfect excuse to leave.

A couple of detectives in suits that prominently displayed their gold shields came in and looked right at me.

"What are you doing here?"

"I'm doing inspections," I responded nonchalantly.

"Listen, the mayor is coming to sit in this box. You'd better get out of here."

They probably caught on to my act because there really was no reason for me to sit and stay in the box during rounds of "inspection." So, I did the only thing I could do at the time.

"Ok, guys. Thanks a lot. I'll see you later." I got out of there quickly so I could look for another skybox to get into.

I walked around the upper ring where all the skyboxes were located. I turned door knobs and walked in to see what was going on in each one. I kept running into people who looked like stuffed shirts, there only because it was the kind of event that people with money should go to—not because they were really interested in the game itself. I couldn't crash with those people. They seemed more interested in business and that was really a waste of seats. However, after opening about three or four more doors, my firefighter's nose picked up on a smell that let me know I had found a home.

I didn't smell fire, but I smelled pot. I immediately knew that no one in this room was going to get upset with me because I hadn't been invited or didn't have a ticket. I walked in and closed the door. Six or seven guys turned around with their doobies and joints in hand. Suddenly, a look of fear entered their eyes.

"He's a cop!" yelled one of them.

"No, no, no, no!" I reassured them. "I'm not a cop. It's cool. Everything is cool. Who cares? Hey guys, I have a problem. Is it alright if I hang out with you? I'm kind of doing this building inspection and the game is about to start."

"Yeah! Come on in! Have a drink! Do what you want. No problem."

Now that I had a spot, I put my shopping bag and clipboard to the side. There I was, partying with guys in seats that may have cost $10,000 or more. I didn't know. But these were young Wall Street guys in their mid-thirties, and they were really partying. They ordered all this food and all these drinks. I couldn't tell you what it cost, but they partied the whole time.

I had told a few people in my firehouse, Ladder 148, that I was going to get into the game that night. I didn't tell them how, but I just knew I was going to get in. So, when I saw the phone in the skybox, I called up the firehouse.

"Do you hear this?" I asked the firefighter who answered the phone just before I turned the receiver so that it could pick up all the screaming from the fans who filled the Garden.

When I put the phone back to my ear, I heard Bobby Perretta shouting to everyone around him.

"He's in the game! I can't believe it. He's in the game!"

They were all really happy for me. I couldn't tell them how I'd done it, though.

The game was a nail-biter. Near the end, the Rangers were up by one goal. I decided it was time for me to make a move.

"Hey, guys. I'm going to take off my uniform and put it in this bag. You give me one of your cards so I can reach you later."

I was at the top of the Garden, so to reach the ice I had to run down the emergency exit with my skates on, with a minute left in the game. I decided to put on my jersey over my uniform so that I would make it in time. I put my shoes and my hat in the bag. When the guys saw my jersey, they went crazy over it. After I told them my plan for getting my hands on the Stanley Cup to represent all the New York fans, they volunteered to be my backup.

"If you get locked up, we'll bail you out. Don't worry about it!"

I hadn't thought about that outcome before they'd said it and I could have lived without them mentioning it, but I didn't let it sway me from my mission. I ran all the way down to the first level using the emergency exit stairwell. Then I approached the glass that was low enough for me to jump over when I noticed something that I hadn't anticipated.

This was the first year that Mayor Giuliani was in office and he had ordered the riot police to be placed all around the ice just before the end of the game to keep everything in check. People go crazy after Stanley Cup games. In some cities, people loot, blow up stuff...all kinds of things tend to happen, so he had taken the precautions he thought necessary to keep everything in order. There must have been about 200 of them. I still tried to edge closer to the ice. I finally got within fifteen feet of the glass and then waited because my plan was to go out there after the Cup came out. People all around me screamed and I was ready to get out on the ice and celebrate.

I didn't care that the cops were there because I knew once I got out on the ice with my skates, they wouldn't be able to chase me with their shoes on. They would fly all over the place. I just had to get over that glass. I was going to be one of the first guys to get his hand on that Cup because we deserved it. I was a die-hard Rangers fan, not to mention the best fan in Madison Square Garden, and this was as good as it got. My plan was, the next night, to either be on David Letterman or be in jail. In either case, I was going to get my hands on that Cup.

While I was lost in my thoughts about what to do next, I didn't realize that I was standing next to the NYPD lieutenant in charge of the section where I was standing. A small detail of guys was with him. Something about me caught his attention because he kept watching me. I tried to look forward nonchalantly like I didn't feel him looking at me, but when he finally looked down, my entire plan was ruined.

"He's got skates on!"

At this point, I was eight to ten feet away but before I could even make a move toward the glass, about four or five big cops grabbed me and threw me on the ground. They didn't know if I was a terrorist or some other kind of crazy man. They only knew that I had worn skates and that I had planned something that probably wouldn't be good news for them or their jobs. Once they pinned me down to the ground, they started rifling through my pockets.

"What's that?" one asked.

"That's my badge."

"Your badge? You're a cop?"

"No, I'm a firefighter."

"Hey, Lou. This guy's a dopey firefighter."

The lieutenant told them to stand me up so he could talk to me.

"There's no way you're getting on the ice. I'm getting promoted to captain in a short while and this will be a tremendous stain on my record if you jump on the ice. You can stand there. I'm going to have all these cops stand around you. But if you make a move, I'm going to handcuff you and lock you up. No matter what!"

So, I patiently waited a few extra minutes to watch them bring out the Stanley Cup. It was beautiful and I still enjoyed watching my team celebrate our victory. When I walked outside, everybody was happy. There was no violence whatsoever. Everybody was hugging and high-fiving each other. I was ecstatic too!

I was still walking around in my ice skates because I had lost my shoes and my hat. I didn't lose the card I had grabbed from one of the guys, but I didn't remember how to get back to the skybox I'd been in earlier, and I didn't know the skybox phone number so I could check on retrieving my belongings. I'd had more than a few beers in me at the time, but I wasn't driving home and nothing at all seemed to matter. All the nearby bars were emptied, which flooded the streets with thousands of additional revelers. Part two of this enchanted evening was about to start.

So many people were celebrating on the Madison Square Garden plaza and in the street that I stopped several times to dance with, hug, or chest bump everyone I met. Drivers and passengers left empty cars and taxis in a traffic jam in the street while they joined the fans in celebration. The air was filled with chants, laughter, song, and the sounds of hundreds of popping champagne bottles.

I danced on 8th Avenue in my ice skates while chanting "1940," and, "Let's Go Rangers!"

One fan's sign said it all: "NOW I CAN DIE IN PEACE." I had the best time of my life and it was one of the greatest things I've ever done.

But since September 11th, I've gained a newfound passion that I'm even more determined to pursue than my goal of watching the New York Rangers play in a final game seven and win the all-too-elusive

Stanley Cup. I'm determined to make sure that people don't forget the sacrifice and significance of September 11th, 2001 and the lessons we can learn from it on how we live our own lives.

What can we learn from 9/11?

As a nation, America almost fell apart with the devastation and destruction of the World Trade Center's two 110-story buildings and five other buildings, the destruction and demolition of the surrounding neighborhood, the disruption and shutting down of the New York City Stock Exchange, the annihilation and vaporization of more than one hundred long-established businesses, and the sorrow created by the existence of broken families and missing loved ones. Fear and sadness still overwhelm me when I think about the unshakable and never-ending punishment and the tragic disappointment that fell on me when I returned to Dante's Inferno in those days, weeks, and months following September 11th. For some time, I lived in Hell. By day, I was a reverse gravedigger, looking for survivors. By night, I was a zombie that wouldn't—and couldn't—sleep.

Imagine living with the hope of recovering a small remnant or the pulverized and withered fragment of a human cadaver that not too long ago had belonged to a living and loving human. We hoped for a miraculous rescue by anyone at any time. We hoped that just one person would be found alive, possibly in a vault or in the safety of some other small crevice in the bowels of the building. Then we would watch as, over time, the hope of finding someone alive diminished into the vaporous, ashy fog of what still remained.

As a proud American citizen, I share this loss with every American who was alive on that day. Yet, this wasn't the only loss I experienced in response to that day. My career nosedived into obscurity. It had been a career that I thought I would continue for at least another twenty years. I had aspirations of passing the test to become an officer—a lieutenant.

After that, I planned to learn, teach, and study a few more years so that I could become a captain or even, possibly someday, a chief before I reached that second-tier of another twenty-year plateau. What had once been a possibility was now an impossibility. Talk about a game-changer. I had been blindsided and my heart hung heavy—too heavy to quit. I wasn't a quitter. I'll never be a quitter, but my career was in the toilet. My world as I knew it had been ripped out from under me.

I lived out the next few years working in total obscurity on Staten Island. Staten Island was the land of very few structural fires, the kinds of fires I was groomed to handle. Staten Island was the home of car accidents and brush fires. I was no longer "Hammer." I had become Smokey the Bear.

I got the nickname "Hammer" from fellow Trucker Wayne Smith while I worked with him in Ladder 4 in Manhattan. He gave me the name when he noted that I was a good *irons man* and that I could hit the hell out of a softball. I guess the name fit because it stuck with me throughout my career. I was officially the "Hammer."

It wasn't a bad moniker. Many firefighters had shitty nicknames over which they had no control. You didn't pick your own nickname. You earned it, one way or another. I definitely came across some regrettable monikers whose owners passionately hated them: Cock-a-Pants, Booze Bag, Hair Bag, Square Rooter, Seagull, Space Cadet, Pugsley and Fresh Air Man.

These names occasionally caused an uproar, leading to threats, fisticuffs, stabbings and sometimes all-out war within the house. Unofficial sit-downs were necessary to restore house order. The sit-downs were attended only by company members; officers were never involved. The senior men who had been in that house the longest ran the show and were the highest in the pecking order.

I miss my brother Wayne Smith. Wayne was big, strong, and

very intelligent. He was also a Detroit Tigers fan. I could never figure out that one, as he was a kid from Queens and lived a stone's throw from Shea Stadium, surrounded by a borough of very loyal Mets fans. Wayne, who was six-foot-four and weighed 220 pounds, was a soft-handed first baseman who batted lefty. He had been a pitcher at St. John's University, also known for its great basketball program and fine baseball team. New York Mets Hall of Fame pitcher John Franco also attended St. John's.

As a firefighter, Wayne rose to the rank of lieutenant very quickly. I don't think he had fifteen years on the job before he earned that rank. This was a pretty amazing accomplishment and he certainly earned his promotion. But Captain Wayne Smith was killed in a hellacious fire on August 7, 1994 in the borough where he'd been born: Queens, New York. I visited him at the burn center in Manhattan after his wife and family had left. Wayne was never left alone; twenty-four hours a day, someone was by his side. I was met by Lieutenant Mike McGlocklin, affectionately known as Opie when the three of us worked together as firefighters at Ladder Company 4. Now Opie was a lieutenant in Ladder 138 in Queens. One of our brothers stood vigil. There was always someone from his house of Engine 287, Ladder 136 as well as Engine 54, Ladder 4, Battalion 9 and the house of Engine 205, Ladder 110 where Wayne served as a lieutenant.

Opie had warned me before I entered the sterile setting of Wayne's room. I was shocked and I froze when I saw my good friend lying there. I saw what fire could do to even us, the well-trained. Wayne's face and head were burned and swollen beyond recognition. Wayne was a courageous fighter who fought to live. He fought and lingered for forty days, never opening his eyes from that terrible coma. Wayne finally succumbed because the noxious superheated air and flames had seared his lungs on the inside, causing irreversible damage. Wayne's fight had been fought.

Wayne's deadly fire was critiqued by the FDNY investigations unit. The conclusion was that Wayne could have saved himself many times throughout that job, but that he, as captain of Ladder 110, simply chose not to. Captain Wayne Smith had led his men into that raging inferno. He had pushed through the deadly flames even after his mask was depleted of air, making matters critical and deadly. Without regard for the flames and searing heat, Captain Wayne Smith had stayed and searched for one of his unaccounted members who, unbeknownst to Wayne, had already escaped.

If you'd ever had the pleasure of meeting Wayne Smith, you soon would have seen that beyond his rugged exterior was a man who would quietly lay down his life for you. I was honored to be named "The Hammer" by Wayne Smith, who is now the starting pitcher for Heaven's Detroit Tigers. But then I had been reduced from being a high-rise firefighter in Manhattan and an accomplished, seasoned firefighter in the borough of fire—Brooklyn, New York—to becoming a mere shell of myself, exiled from the world I knew and sent to the borough of Staten Island.

Until I found another purpose, I thought my life was over. Unfortunately, I am not the only person who has found himself in a situation in which his life as he knew it was suddenly facing an attack that he could never have predicted.

We all heal in different ways. I am a very sensitive person and I don't think I will ever completely heal.

I will NEVER FORGET the attacks of September 11th or their aftermath, which changed my career. Both still create many emotions and great pain and suffering to this day.

According to the FDNY Medical Division information at the time of writing this third edition, almost 200 NYC firefighters who have died of respiratory illnesses and cancer caused by exposure during the

Ground Zero rescue and recovery. Even Billy O'Connor died of cancer about five years after the day we worked together pulling people from the rubble. This is something I will carry with me until God calls me to Heaven as a good and faithful soul, but even this is not the full extent of the impact:

- there are over 800 9/11 related deaths of police officers, military personnel and civilians who lived in the area, and thousands more are suffering with related stress and health issues,

- according to the 9/11 Memorial Museum as of the time of this writing, 19,500 body parts were collected to date, and only 1,102 were identified,

- 1,616 families received death certificates without a body to bury, and

- more than 3,000 children lost their parents, and the average of the children who lost a parent was eight years old.

Not to mention the start of having TSA security at every airport in the country, the full impact of that day goes far beyond this list. Even now, I see oncologists and dermatologists and other specialists who are monitoring my condition and health issues as they evolve over time. I also continue to be treated for post-traumatic stress disorder or PTSD.

Through all of this, I have learned three things that help me move forward.

1. **Use whatever God has blessed you with to help and benefit someone else.** Whether it's a special talent that can help others, money, a unique personality, or even your ability to physically help someone. Continuing to adopt children in foreign countries through World Vision, being part of the security team at a summer camp for children with cancer through the Optimist Club, sharing my story as a docent at the

Tribute Center, and speaking at several 9/11 memorial events over the years have gone a long way toward helping me make sense of what happened and giving me a new outlook on future possibilities. Since publishing the first edition of this book, I've been on field at NFL games when they remember 9/11, introduced underprivileged children in charter schools and academies throughout the United States to the events and after math of 9/11, I've spoken to several groups about the lessons we can all learn about recovering from devastating life events, and I've revised my goal of build a 9/11 museum in Florida to building traveling 9/11 museum to help us *all* never forget.

2. **Remember that someone else's unfortunate life is much worse and graver than yours. Thank God that you have the voice and ability to change your life for the better.** As devastated as I was at the loss of my career, Welles Crowther was an incredible man who never had the chance to complete his career change from an equity trader to a firefighter. At least I had the chance to enjoy my dream career for twenty years, and I still have my life today so that I can continue reaching for new dreams.

3. **Never give up. Move in a positive direction by taking just one step at a time. Seek professional help if necessary.** I didn't want to start seeing a psychologist, but I still see one today to help me stay balanced. It is a decision that I will never regret.

Children Are Our Future

For the past five or six years, I have invested my time and dime into visiting underprivileged young adults aged twelve to twenty-two in some of the most dangerous cities in America—Detroit, St. Paul and Miami to name a few. When I go to speak about an event that happened before many of them were born, I imagine them wondering who this old white guy is and how could I possibly relate to their lives as minorities in cities better known for their crime stats than any tourist destinations.

I was blessed with the love, protection and provision of both my parents and a close bond with my brothers, but it was no walk in the park for me growing up either. As you may remember, I hardly saw my mom and dad between the ages of five and eight-and-a-half because they spent most of their non-working hours beside my baby sister's hospital bed while she fought leukemia. Attending my baby sister's wake, funeral and burial just days before Christmas engraved scars into my childhood that run painfully deep.

I don't pretend that my story is the same as theirs, but in my own way I can relate to many of these bright minded young people that have not ever been given a fair chance. I start by telling them that my day has already come and gone. The best of me has passed by, and if it weren't for the grace of God I would not be standing in front of them.

Then I look a few of them straight in the eye, "the future of America is you and you and you and you." I strongly believe they can achieve anything they put their mind to when we offer a helping hand, some love, direction, morals, truth and honesty.

I tell the students that God's master plan includes our happy, successful and loving lives, and if God has given you a special talent you must use it. If you are an artist, a musician, a dancer, an athlete or have other exceptional skills in areas such as mathematics, science or poetry, you should pursue that wonderful gift by all means. Don't ever worry about money. When you do what you love to do, you will do well. If someone says you can't, I know and I am telling you that you can. You will be happy and the money will follow.

Then I explain the history of the World Trade Center, just as I explained it to you in the introduction, and narrate my story as a New York City firefighter using my PowerPoint presentation of what I saw at Ground Zero the morning of September 11, 2001. For the most part, the students were astounded by my story of what unfolded that day. Their eyes followed me intensively as I walked back and forth discussing and pointing out the many things in front of them on the screen. You could've heard a pin drop. Remarkably, I held their complete and utter attention for almost an hour—not one of them ever looked down to fuss with his own mobile device. Many of them had tears in their eyes, and at one point a young girl was shaking and crying so hard that I went over and gave her the big hug she so desperately needed. Eventually, she was able to sit down have a sip of water and regain control of her thoughts and emotions.

At one point I thought maybe they don't even have their cell phones with them, but after I completed my presentation they all pulled out their cell phones and asked to take photos with me. My hope is that the photo wasn't the only thing they walked away with. I hope they also walked away understanding who I was before 9/11, who I became after and how deeply I care for each and every one of them.

Before everyone leaves, I ask for one favor. "There were young people—as young or younger than you—who have given their life to protect our nation in wartime so that we may live in peace, safety and, most of all, freedom—which most of the world does not have. We live in the greatest country in the world. Many people from all over the world are dying to come into our nation: the United States of America. As a gesture in remembrance of these brave young people from all over our country of all different races, colors, beliefs who gave their live so you can live yours, please—I beg you—please remember to vote at every election. Your vote counts as much as anyone else's because others gave their lives for you to have the rights and the freedom we continuously enjoy. I don't care who you vote for. Vote for who you believe in, who you trust or who you dislike the least. The changing of the guard takes place after each election, and you will impact the changing."

I'm always grateful and satisfied to share the truth about September 11, 2001. I reinforce this by telling them I was not a very good student in high school and I barely passed my English classes. although as I raise my hand up and display my book "Chiefs, Pawns & Warriors."

I clearly tell them that if I can write this book, which is featured in the 9/11 Memorial Museum in New York City, then they can achieve anything.

In life, we all have the choice to be a chief, a pawn, or a warrior. In some instances you may be a chief and in others you may never want to shoulder that kind of leadership responsibility…and that's fine. You may never want to be a warrior but a time may come when you rise to the occasion and masterfully transform into the hidden warrior who's within you, like thousands of us on the search-and-rescue team did following September 11th, or even as I did when I started the process of shrugging off my depression long enough to start becoming an active participant in life again.

You may have been led to believe that being a pawn is less desirable than the other two roles. Believe me, being a pawn can be a wonderful thing. When you learn to be at peace with yourself and find contentment in where you are, you realize that this is a place where the warriors and chiefs around you are actively protecting you. This was my role during much of my career as a firefighter. We always went into dangerous situations, but because I was part of a great team whose chiefs and warriors stepped up as needed, my life as a pawn was always protected and my work helped the chiefs and warriors do a better job of protecting me. The same is true for you.

It is your God-given choice to determine when and how you'll transition between the roles because all are necessary to reach our life goals. Through hard work, determination, skill, knowledge, perseverance, and drive, you will succeed and achieve your ultimate goal.

I know that I am all three: a chief, a pawn, and a warrior. For the most part, I'm a pawn now in a relaxed state of mind —just relaxing and learning new things. Part of the reason why I am so at ease with being a pawn is that I know I am trained to be a warrior and that I can transform into one at a moment's notice if I have to. Hopefully, I'm not getting too long in the tooth, but I know that a true warrior lies hidden beneath this well-rested body. Too much time has passed for me to aspire to be an FDNY chief, although I have witnessed and studied a great many chiefs in my lifetime. I respectfully thank them for their undaunted professional actions and their perseverance, which has kept the brothers and me safe and alive so that we could return to our families every day. I can't thank them enough. However, I still haven't given up on the thought that I may be required to serve as chief for other missions. If it happens, I'll be ready.

My question for you is this: do you choose to be a chief, a pawn or a warrior? You can tell me your answer in a comment on my website at AuthorRonParker.com. Notice that choosing to be a victim is never an option.

Watch your thoughts for they become words.

Watch your words for they become actions.

Watch your actions for they become habits.

Watch your habits for they become your character.

And watch your character for it becomes your destiny.

What we think, we become.

My father always said that…and I think I am fine.

-Margaret Thatcher

POSTSCRIPT

These are the first responders who we will "Never Forget" for their ultimate sacrifice on September 11, 2001.

RON'S GUYS

This list is according to the official list by the FDNY. Please note that any ranks with an asterisk were awarded posthumously.

FDNY Chief
Peter J. Ganci, Jr.

FDNY Assistant Chief
Gerard Barbara
Donald Burns

FDNY First Deputy Commissioner
William M. Feehan

FDNY Fire Marshal
Ronald Paul Bucca

FDNY Chaplain
Father Mychal Judge

Battalion 4
Chief Matthew Lancelot Ryan

Battalion 2
Chief William McGovern
Chief Richard Prunty
Faustino Apostol, Jr.

Battalion 6
Chief John P. Williamson

Battalion 7
*Deputy Chief Orio Palmer

Battalion 8
Chief Thomas Patrick DeAngelis

Battalion 9
*Deputy Chief Edward F. Geraghty
Chief Dennis Lawrence Devlin
Carl Asaro
Alan D. Feinberg

Battalion 12
*Deputy Chief Joseph Ross Marchbanks, Jr.
Chief Frederick Claude Scheffold, Jr.

Battalion 48
Chief Joseph Grzelak
Michael Leopoldo Bocchino

Battalion 57
*Deputy Chief Dennis Cross

Engine 1
Lt. Andrew Desperito
Michael T. Weinberg

Engine 4
*Chief Joseph D. Farrelly
Calixto Anaya, Jr.
James C. Riches
Thomas G. Schoales
Paul A. Tegtmeier

Engine 5
*Lt. Manuel Del Valle

Engine 6
Paul Beyer
Thomas Holohan
William R. Johnston

Engine 8
Robert Parro

Engine 10
Lt. Gregg Arthur Atlas
*Fire Marshal Paul Pansini
Jeffrey James Olsen

Engine 21
Capt. William Francis Burke, Jr.

Engine 22
*Fire Marshal Vincent D. Kane
Thomas Anthony Casoria
Michael J. Elferis
Martin E. McWilliams

Engine 23
John Marshall
Robert McPadden
James Nicholas Pappageorge
Hector Luis Tirado, Jr.
Mark P. Whitford

Engine 26
*Chief Thomas Farino
Dana R Hannon
Robert W. Spear, Jr.

Engine 33
Lt. Kevin Pfeifer
David Arce
Brian Bilcher
Michael Boyle
Robert Evans
Robert King, Jr.
Keithroy Marcellus Maynard

Engine 37
John Giordano

Engine 40
Lt. John F. Ginley
Kevin Bracken
Michael D. D'Auria

Bruce Gary
Michael Lynch
Steve Mercado

Engine 52
Lt. Thomas O'Hagan

Engine 54
Paul John Gill
Jose Guadalupe
Leonard Ragaglia
Christopher Santora

Engine 55
Lt. Peter L. Freund
Robert Lane
Christopher Mozzillo
Stephen P. Russell

Engine 58
Lt. Robert B. Nagel

Engine 65
Thomas McCann

Engine 74
Ruben D. Correa

Engine 82
Lt. Geoffrey E. Guja

Engine 152
Robert Cordice

Engine 154
Capt. William O'Keefe

Engine 201
Lt. Paul Richard Martini
Greg Joseph Buck
Christopher Pickford
John Albert Schardt

Engine 205
Lt. Robert Francis Wallace

Engine 207
Karl Henry Joseph
Shawn Edward Powell
Kevin O. Reilly

Engine 214
*Lt. Carl John Bedigian
John Joseph Florio
Michael Edward Roberts
Kenneth Thomas Watson

Engine 216
Daniel Suhr

Engine 217
Lt. Kenneth Phelan
Steven Coakley
Philip T. Hayes
Neil Joseph Leavy

Engine 219
John Chipura

Engine 226
Brian McAleese
David Paul Derubbio
Stanley S. Smagala, Jr.

Engine 230
Lt. Brian G. Ahearn
Frank Bonomo
Michael Scott Carlo
Jeffrey Stark
Eugene Whelan
Edward James White III

Engine 235
Lt. Steven Bates
Nicholas Paul Chiofalo
Francis Esposito
Lee S. Fehling
Lawrence G. Veling

Engine 238
Lt. Glenn E. Wilkinson

Engine 279
Ronnie Lee Henderson
Michael Ragusa
Anthony Rodriguez

Engine 285
Raymond R. York

Engine 310
Capt. Thomas Moody

Engine 320
Capt. James J. Corrigan

Haz-Mat 1
Lt. John A. Crisci
Dennis M. Carey
Martin N. DeMeo
Thomas Gardner
Jonathan R. Hohmann
Dennis Scauso
Kevin Joseph Smith
Capt. Patrick J. Waters

Haz-Mat Operations
Battalion Chief John Fanning

Ladder 2
Capt. Frederick Ill, Jr.
Michael J. Clarke
George DiPasquale
Denis P. Germain
Daniel Edward Harlin
Carl Molinaro
Dennis Michael Mulligan

Ladder 3
Capt. Patrick J. Brown
Lt. Kevin W. Donnelly
Michael Carroll
James Raymond Coyle
Gerard Dewan
Jeffrey John Giordano
Joseph Maloney

John Kevin McAvoy
Timothy Patrick McSweeney
Joseph J. Ogren
Steven John Olson

Ladder 4
*Capt. Daniel O'Callaghan
Capt. David Terence Wooley
*Lt. Michael F. Lynch
Joseph Angelini, Jr.
Michael E. Brennan
Michael Haub
Samuel Oitice
John James Tipping II

Ladder 5
*Capt. Vincent Francis Giammona
Lt. Charles Joseph Margiotta
Lt. Michael Warchola
Louis Arena
Andrew Brunn
Thomas Hannafin
Paul Hanlon Keating
John A. Santore
Gregory Thomas Saucedo

Ladder 7
*Capt. Vernon Allan Richard
George Cain
Robert Joseph Foti
Richard Muldowney, Jr.
Charles Mendez
Vincent Princiotta

Ladder 8
Lt. Vincent Gerard Halloran

Ladder 9
*Lt. Jeffrey P. Walz
Gerard Baptiste
John P. Tierney

Ladder 10
Sean Patrick Tallon

Ladder 11
Lt. Michael Quilty
Michael F. Cammarata
Edward James Day
John F. Heffernan
Richard John Kelly, Jr.
Matthew Rogan

Ladder 12
Angel L. Juarbe, Jr.
Michael D. Mullan

Ladder 13
Capt. Walter G. Hynes
Thomas Hetzel
Dennis McHugh
Thomas E. Sabella
Gregory Stajk

Ladder 15
Lt. Joseph Gerard Leavey
Richard Lanard Allen
Arthur Barry
Thomas W. Kelly
Scott Kopytko
Scott Larsen
Douglas E. Oelschlager
Eric T. Olsen

Ladder 16
Lt. Raymond E. Murphy
Robert Curatolo

Ladder 20
*Capt. John R. Fischer
John Patrick Burnside
James Michael Gray
Sean S. Hanley
David Laforge
Robert Thomas Linnane
Robert D. McMahon

Ladder 21
Lt. Michael N. Fodor
Gerald T. Atwood
Gerard Duffy
Keith Glascoe
Joseph Henry
William E. Krukowski
Benjamin Suarez

Ladder 24
Capt. Daniel J. Brethel
Stephen Elliot Belson

Ladder 25
*Fire Marshal Kenneth Kumpel
Matthew Barnes
John Michael Collins
Robert Minara
Joseph Rivelli, Jr.
Paul G. Ruback

Ladder 34
Lt. Anthony Jovic
Lt. Glenn C. Perry

Ladder 35
Capt. Frank Callahan
James Andrew Giberson
Vincent S. Morello
Michael Otten
Michael Roberts

Ladder 42
Peter Alexander Bielfeld

Ladder 61
Lt. Charles William Garbarini

Ladder 101
Lt. Joseph Gullickson
Patrick Byrne
Salvatore B. Calabro
Brian Cannizzaro

Thomas J. Kennedy
Joseph Maffeo
Terence A. McShane

Ladder 103
Capt. Timothy M. Stackpole

Ladder 105
Capt. Vincent Brunton
*Lt. Thomas Richard Kelly
Henry Alfred Miller, Jr.
Dennis O'Berg
Frank Anthony Palombo

Ladder 110
Lt. Paul Thomas Mitchell

Ladder 111
Lt. Christopher P. Sullivan

Ladder 118
Capt. Martin J. Egan, Jr.
Lt. Robert M. Regan
*Lt. Joseph Agnello
Vernon Paul Cherry
Scott Matthew Davidson
Leon Smith, Jr.
Peter Anthony Vega

Ladder 131
Christian Michael Otto Regenhard

Ladder 132
*Battalion Chief Thomas Theodore Haskell, Jr.
Andrew Jordan
Michael Kiefer
Thomas Mingione
John T. Vigiano II
Sergio Villanueva

Ladder 136
Michael Joseph Cawley

Ladder 148
Lt. Philip Scott Petti

Ladder 157
Lt. Stephen G. Harrell

Ladder 166
William X. Wren

Rescue 1
Capt. Terence S. Hatton
Lt. Dennis Mojica
Joseph Angelini, Sr.
Gary Geidel
William Henry
Kenneth Joseph Marino
Michael Montesi
Gerard Terence Nevins
Patrick J. O'Keefe
Brian Edward Sweeney
David M. Weiss

Rescue 2
Lt. Peter C. Martin
*Lt. John Napolitano
William David Lake
Daniel F. Libretti
Kevin O'Rourke
Lincoln Quappe
Edward Rall

Rescue 3
Christopher Joseph Blackwell
Thomas Foley
Thomas Gambino, Jr.
Raymond Meisenheimer
Donald J. Regan
Gerard Patrick Schrang
Joseph Spor

Rescue 4
*Battalion Chief Brian Hickey
Lt. Kevin Dowdell
Terrence Patrick Farrell
William J. Mahoney
Peter Allen Nelson
Durrell V. Pearsall

Rescue 5
*Battalion Chief Louis Joseph Modafferi
Lt. Harvey Harrell
*Fire Marshal Andre G. Fletcher
John P. Bergin
Carl Vincent Bini
Michael Curtis Fiore
Joseph Mascali
Douglas Charles Miller
Jeffrey Matthew Palazzo
Nicholas P. Rossomando
Allan Tarasiewicz

Special Operations
Battalion Chief John Moran
*Deputy Chief Raymond Mathew Downey
*Deputy Chief Charles Kasper
*Deputy Chief John M. Paolillo

Squad 1
*Chief James M. Amato
*Capt. Michael Esposito
Lt. Edward A. D'Atri
*Lt. David J. Fontana
Lt. Michael Thomas Russo, Sr.
Gary Box
Thomas M. Butler
Peter Carroll
Matthew David Garvey
Stephen Gerard Siller

Squad 18
*Capt. William E. McGinn
*Lt. Andrew Fredericks
*Lt. David Halderman
Eric Allen
Timothy Haskell
Manuel Mojica
Lawrence Virgilio

Squad 41
Lt. Michael K. Healey

Thomas Patrick Cullen III
Robert Hamilton
Michael J. Lyons
Gregory Sikorsky
Richard Bruce Van Hine

Squad 252
Lt. Timothy Higgins
*Lt. Patrick Lyons
Tarel Coleman
Thomas Kuveikis
Peter J. Langone
Kevin Prior

Squad 288
*Lt. Ronnie E. Gies
Lt. Ronald T. Kerwin
Peter Brennan
Joseph Hunter
Jonathan Lee Ielpi
Adam David Rand
Timothy Matthew Welty

EMS Battalion 49
Paramedic Carlos R. Lillo

EMS Battalion 57
*EMS Lt. Ricardo J. Quinn

Safety Battalion 1
Chief Lawrence T. Stack
Robert Crawford

New York Fire Patrol
Keith M. Roma, Fire Patrol 2

DAD'S GUYS

New York City Police Department (NYPD)
Sgt. Timothy A. Roy, Sr.
Sgt. John Gerard Coughlin
Sgt. Rodney C. Gillis
Sgt. Michael S. Curtin
Det. Joseph V. Vigiano

Det. Claude Daniel Richards
Moira Ann Smith
Ramon Suarez
Paul Talty
Santos Valentin, Jr.
Walter E. Weaver
Ronald Philip Kloepfer
Thomas M. Langone
James Patrick Leahy
Brian Grady McDonnell
John William Perry
Glen Kerrin Pettit
John D'Allara
Vincent Danz
Jerome M. P. Dominguez
Stephen P. Driscoll
Mark Joseph Ellis
Robert Fazio, Jr.

MIKE'S GUYS

Port Authority Police Department (PAPD)
Supt. Ferdinand V. Morrone
Chief James A. Romito
Lt. Robert D. Cirri
Insp. Anthony P. Infante, Jr.
Capt. Kathy Nancy Mazza
Sgt. Robert M. Kaulfers
Donald James McIntyre
Walter Arthur McNeil
Joseph Michael Navas
James Nelson
Alfonse J. Niedermeyer
James Wendell Parham
Dominick A. Pezzulo
Antonio J. Rodrigues
Richard Rodriguez
Bruce Albert Reynolds
Christopher C. Amoroso
Maurice V. Barry

Clinton Davis, Sr.
Donald A. Foreman
Gregg J. Froehner
Uhuru Gonga Houston
George G. Howard
Thomas E. Gorman
Stephen Huczko, Jr.
Paul William Jurgens
Liam Callahan
Paul Laszczynski
David Prudencio Lemagne
John Joseph Lennon, Jr.
John Dennis Levi
James Francis Lynch
John P. Skala
Walwyn W. Stuart, Jr.
Kenneth F. Tietjen
Nathaniel Webb
Michael T. Wholey

Made in the USA
Columbia, SC
05 August 2019